AMONG all the books published on Henry James and his work during the past twenty-five years, but a precious few can be said to come to terms with him as a major phenomenon in English culture: this book is one of that few. It is a brilliant and subtle demonstration of James's use of money as the principal symbol of the essential epistemological meanings at the heart of his major fiction.

The initial chapters consider James's ambiguous attitude toward money and his tentative modulations of the financial motif in the early short stories and novels. The two central chapters of the book are given over to meticulous analyses of *The Portrait of a Lady* and *The Golden Bowl,* those novels that, Mr. Mull contends, most fully show James's concept of property as the symbol for both the potentialities of the individual self and for that seemingly intractable world in which these potentialities may be realized. A concluding chapter examines *The Ivory Tower* and *The American Scene.*

An example of literary criticism at its best, this first book by Mr. Mull will be of great interest to scholars of American literature and to all readers of Henry James.

HENRY JAMES'S 'SUBLIME ECONOMY'

Henry James's 'Sublime Economy'

MONEY AS SYMBOLIC CENTER

IN THE FICTION

by DONALD L. MULL

WESLEYAN UNIVERSITY PRESS

Middletown, Connecticut

The poem 'Theory' by Wallace Stevens, which is quoted on page 48, is reprinted from *The Collected Poems* by permission of Alfred A. Knopf, Inc. Copyright 1923; renewed 1951 by Wallace Stevens.

The publisher gratefully acknowledges the support of the Andrew W. Mellon Foundation toward the publication of this book.

Library of Congress Cataloging in Publication Data

Mull, Donald L   1936–
    Henry James's 'sublime economy'.

    Bibliography: p. [188]- 191,
    1. James, Henry, 1843–1916.   2. Money in literature.
I. Title.
PS2127.M6M8   813'.4   73–6007
ISBN 0–8195–4064–1

Manufactured in the United States of America
First edition

To the R and the Etta

Contents

Acknowledgements

I wish to express thanks to R. W. B. Lewis, who directed the writing of the dissertation from which the present work grew, and to Charles N. Feidelson, Jr., with whom I first studied James intensively; to James H. Wheatley and George R. Creeger, who provided valuable criticism concerning substance and structure, and to Steven Zwicker, who gave sound stylistic advice; to Fran Tallman, my invaluable research assistant; and ultimately to Ruthe and Martin Battestin, Fred Bornhauser, Sam Carmack, Richard Greer, Anne Kiley, Markesan Morrison, the late Bob Orr, Stuart Riggsby, Alan Shavzin, Max Wickert, Viola Winner—even Martha Stephens—and the many other friends whose conversations have illuminated James for me.

ABBREVIATIONS

The following abbreviations are used in indicating the sources of quotations from James's works. The editions cited are listed in the bibliography.

Am	The American
ANS	The American Novels and Stories of Henry James
AS	The American Scene
Eur	The Europeans
EUT	Eight Uncollected Tales of Henry James
GB	The Golden Bowl
LP	A Landscape Painter
ME	Master Eustace
MF	The Madonna of the Future
NSB	Notes of a Son and Brother
NY	The Novels and Tales of Henry James
	The New York Edition
PL	The Portrait of a Lady
RH	Roderick Hudson
SBO	A Small Boy and Others
SR	Sories Revived
TC	Travelling Companions
WW	Watch and Ward

HENRY JAMES'S 'SUBLIME ECONOMY'

Biographical

IN *Notes of a Son and Brother* the seventy-year-old Henry James recaptures from his remote past a scene emblematic of his imaginative and artistic nature. The occasion, in comparison to the more celebrated epiphanies in the history of this artist's imagination—the discovery of "Europe" in the juxtaposition of an old peasant woman and a ruined castle, or the confrontation with the "other self" in the dream of the Louvre (*SBO*, 159–161, 195–197)—seems rather pedestrian, merely a young writer's first success in selling his work; but it is, at least in the mature author's rendering of it, as significant as its more patently suggestive fellows in presenting a complex of attitude and meaning central to the whole canon of Henry James.

What simply happened was that Charles Eliot Norton had accepted an unsigned review of Nassau W. Senior's *Essays on Fiction*—the first appearance in print of Henry James, Jr.[1] James, however, recalls the event thus:

> I see before me, in the rich, the many-hued light of my room . . . the very greenbacks, to the total value of twelve dollars, into which I had changed the checque representing my first earned wage. I had earned it, I couldn't but feel, with fabulous felicity: a circumstance so strangely mixed with the fact that literary composition of a high order had, at that very table where the greenbacks were spread out, quite viciously declined, and with the air of its being also once for all, to "come" on any save its own essential terms, which it seemed to distinguish in the most invidious manner conceivable from mine. It was to insist through all my course on this distinction, and sordid gain thereby never again to seem so easy as in that prime handling of my fee. (*NSB*, 476)

At the center of the scene are the twelve greenbacks, upon which plays "the rich, the many-hued light," the characteristic Jamesian ambiguity of presentation. The central image of the money becomes a focal point at which converge and from which reflect the conflicting attitudes of the author evinced by the scene—the young writer's elation at having earned his first wage from his craft and the older writer's revulsion at the fact of "sordid gain" (the bluntness of the phrase considerably qualified by that delicate irony which is almost never absent from James's *Autobiography*); the felt felicity of the early composition and the contrasting sense of the disparity between an imposed ideal of "literary composition" and the author's own craft. The method is associational, but everything refers back to and takes its meaning from the image of the money. The conjunction of "literary composition of a high order" and "that very table where the greenbacks were spread out" insists on the relation of the artistic imagination to money, just as it insists on their essential opposition.

If the passage emphasizes James's difficulty in reconciling his art with "sordid gain," the remainder of the paragraph indicates a sense in which the two can be rendered compatible. James proceeds to recall Norton's hospitality following his acceptance of the review:

> I was to grow fond of regarding as a positive consecration to letters that half-hour in the long library at Shady Hill, where the winter sunshine touched serene bookshelves and arrayed pictures, the whole embrowned composition of objects in my view, with I knew not what golden light of promise, what assurance of things to come: there was to be nothing exactly like it later on—the conditions of perfect rightness for a certain fresh felicity, certain decisive pressures of the spring, *can* occur, it would seem, but once. This was on the other hand the beginning of so many intentions that it mattered little if the particular occasion was not repeated; for what did I do again and again, through all the years, but handle in plenty what I might have called the small change of it? (NSB, 477)

The "rich, the many-hued light" of James's room becomes the "golden light of promise" of unknown "things to come," of the possibilities for artistic experience suggested by the conjunction of his first publication and his admission into the literary world. The highly connotative terms associated with money ("rich" and "golden") are taken out of the context of "wage" and "gain" to symbolize, as the light bathing the scene in which the young writer realizes them, the ambiguous potentialities of the imagination. The metaphor becomes overt in the final sentence of the paragraph. The realization of intentions there begun, the fulfilment of the possibilities there glimpsed—these are the "small change" of the "golden light of promise," the fortune of the imagination.

James gradually modulates these terms so that they continually gain nuances of meaning and connote a developing series of attitudes. One can say less that money symbolizes a given particular than that the emotive terms associated with money—ranging from highly favorable ("rich," "golden") to extremely prejorative ("sordid gain")—are brought into significant relation with a complex of varying attitudes (possibly, but not necessarily, attitudes toward the fact of money itself). The image becomes a nexus of meanings, significant in the totality of its relations, rather than a thing determinately meaningful in itself. Abstracting along the lines indicated by the opposed emotive terms we can refer to a commercial and an imaginative sense of money, and indeed, such a distinction proves extremely useful for describing contrasting sets of attitudes in the novels and stories. We must, however, maintain, especially when considering the extremely dense late works, that money is primarily an organic center rather than a thing of fixed aspects.

"If the critics have charged Henry James with being ignorant of the world of business, he largely has himself to blame," remarks Jan W. Dietrichson, who cites the *Autobiography* as the primary source of critical misconception.[2] It is equally true that the *Autobiography* provides the fullest documentation available of James's awareness of the ambiguous fact of money and the sources of that awareness in his father's "ideas." From his own father's world of material acquisition and restricted imagination,[3] Henry James, Sr., had turned to the world of spiritual and imaginative experience, though it was the fruits of his father's acquisitions which permitted him freedom in exploring that world. That complete alienation of the James family from the realm of business which was its base the novelist recorded in *A Small Boy and Others*:

> The most that could be said of us was that, though about equally wanting, all round, in any faculty of acquisition, we happened to pay for the amiable weakness less in some connections than in others. The point was that we moved so oddly and consistently—as it was our only form of consistency—over our limited pasture, never straying to nibble in the strange or the steep places. What was the matter with us under this spell, and what the moral might have been for our case, are issues of small moment, after all, in face of the fact of our mainly so brief duration. It was given to but few of us to be taught by the event, to be made to wonder with the last intensity what *had* been the matter. This it would be interesting to worry out, might I take the time; for the story wouldn't be told, I conceive, by any mere rueful glance at other avidities, the preference for ease, the play of the passions, the appetite for pleasure. These things have often accompanied the business imagination; just as the love of life and the love of other persons, and of many of the things of the world, just as quickness of soul and sense, have again and again not excluded it. However, it comes back, as I have already hinted, to the manner in which the "things of the world" could but present themselves; there were not enough of these, and they were not fine and fair enough, to engage happily so much unapplied, so much loose and crude attention. We hadn't doubtless at all a complete play of intelligence—if I may not so far discriminate as to say *they* hadn't; or our lack of the instinct of the market needn't have been so much worth speaking of: other curiosities, other sympathies might have redressed the balance. (*SBO*, 109–110)

At a loss to account fully for his family's total estrangement from the world of business, its complete lack of the "business imagination," the elderly novelist suggests that the "things of the world" were neither plentiful nor "fine and fair enough" to provide significant material for the overactive imagination of his young self. "Convert, convert, convert!" (*SBO*, 123) the elder Henry James had in effect urged his children; and as Robert Le Clair comments, "It was not into gold that they were to convert their experiences. Of that sort of 'success' in life they never heard a word at home, it being a presumption of their parents that they would hear word enough of that idea elsewhere."[4] The things of the world as such were objects of the business imagination, mere "things," unconverted and thoroughly in "the world." Presenting themselves as things (the manner in which, says James, they necessarily presented themselves), they would hardly fail not to satisfy the demands of the creative imagination, the opposite of the business imagination.

James's slight bafflement in explaining away his lack of interest in or understanding of the world of business amounts finally to his failure to recognize, or at least to state, clearly that the mode of thought which he calls the "business imagination" is completely alien to, antithetical to his own mode of thought, the "converting imagination" inculcated in him by his father, which he later analyzed in *A Small Boy and Others*:

> As I reconsider both my own and my brother's early start . . . it is quite for me as if the authors of our being and guardians of our youth had virtually said to us but one thing, directed our course but by one word, though constantly repeated: Convert, convert, convert! With which I have not even the sense of any needed appeal in us for further apprehension of the particular precious metal our chemistry was to have in view. I taste again in that pure air no ghost of a hint, for instance, that the precious metal was the refined gold of "success"— a reward of effort for which I remember to have heard at home no good word, nor any sort of word, ever faintly breathed. . . . We were to convert and convert, success—in the sense that was in the general air—or no success; and simply everything that should happen to us, every contact, every impression and every experience we should know, were to form our soluble stuff; with only ourselves to thank should we remain unaware, by the time our perceptions were decently developed, of the substance finally projected and most desirable. That substance might be just consummately Virtue, as a social grace and value —and as a matter furthermore on which pretexts for ambiguity

of view and of measure were as little as possible called upon to flourish. This last luxury therefore quite failed us, and we understood no whit the less what was suggested and expected because of the highly liberal way in which the pill, if I may call it so, was gilded: it had been made up—to emphasize my image—in so bright an air of humanity and gaiety, of charity and humour. (*SBO*, 122–123)

Experience was not to be converted into gold; "success" in the world's terms was not what the elder Henry James prescribed for his children, since that would mean, essentially, being converted by the world. Such an attitude, the business imagination, maintained an aggrandizing relationship between the self and the world's things, in which the self was defined by the things it possessed, its appurtenances. Rather, the James children were to convert (the paternal dictum itself "gilded" by the father's humanity) their experience of the world into "Virtue, as a social grace and value" (James's statement of the unambiguity of which is sufficiently ambiguous), a quality of the self permitting it the fullest efficacy in social relations, that is, promoting a rightness of relation with other selves.[5] The elder James's advocated alchemy was, rather than a conversion of experience of the world into the hard fact of gold, a conversion of that fact into another kind of experience, the sort of conversion which his own father's money had undergone at his hands.

In his attempt to isolate the reason for his lack of business sense, James lists several possible alternatives to that sense which —though he finds them possibly concomitant with it and though he rejects them as the causes of his disinterest—suggest certain affinities with the converting imagination and the kinds of relations with persons and things implied by such an imagination. James brackets "the love of life and the love of other persons, and of many of the things of the world, . . . quickness of soul and sense," as things which "have again and again not excluded" the business imagination, the implication being that they generally do. The linking of the love of things with the love of life and the love of persons suggests here not so much an objectification of persons as a personification of objects—a common relation of the self to life, persons, things, whereby the things of the world are not accepted in the terms wherein they present themselves (their business value, their thingness) but are imaginatively apprehended (the most notable exemplar of such an apprehension being Fleda Vetch in *The Spoils of Poynton*), just as other selves are actually apprehended in a true "love of" them. Conversely, if one is related to things in their thingness—if one possesses, that is, the business imagination— one's relation to other persons will generally parallel one's rela- tions to things; people will become commercial entities, objects possessed by one's self, and, as possessions, the concrete defini- tions of the self. The business imagination is thus an attitude toward all aspects of life, an attitude which determines the self's loss in its appurtenances and relations. So Henry James, Sr., treats the concept of owning in "Socialism and Civilization": "We degrade by owning and just in the degree of our owning. . . . We degrade and disesteem every person we own absolutely, every person bound to us by any other tenure than his own spontaneous affection."[6] And this belief of the father's became central in the son's great novels.

Another set of possible alternatives to the business imagi- nation James lists as "other avidities, the preference for ease, the play of the passions, the appetite for pleasure." These, leading as they do to immediate satisfaction of the self in the things and persons of the world rather than to a right relation with other selves and externals, may be seen as the obverse of the convert- ing imagination. They are opposed to the business sense in that money is their condition rather than their end; but viewed in regard to the relation of the self and others, they imply the same attitude as the business sense. The avid, the lovers of ease and pleasure, differ from the business-minded only in that they spend money instead of making it. Early in *A Small Boy and Others*, James describes the implications for the world of *not* being in business:

Not to have been immediately launched in business of a rigor-

ous sort was to be exposed—in the absence I mean of some
fairly abnormal predisposition to virtue; since it was a world
so simply constituted that whatever wasn't business, or exactly
an office or a "store," places in which people sat close and
made money, was just simply pleasure, sought, and sought
only, in places in which people got tipsy. There was clearly
no mean, least of all the golden one, for it was just the ready,
even when the moderate, possession of gold that determined,
that hurried on, disaster. (*SBO*, 30)

To have money instead of making it was, in the eyes of the
world, necessarily to use it wrongly. Leisure and ease led inevitably to pleasure-seeking, and pleasure was not to be sought. One
could always seek more money. James never completely rejects
the possible validity of such an attitude, but its scope, in these
terms, is essentially that of Henrietta Stackpole when she
objects to Ralph Touchett because he doesn't "do" anything.
(Mrs. Touchett, however, who finds her son a failure on the
same grounds, is an example of what Henrietta is, or should be,
driving at, and to an extent is a vindication of Henrietta's point
of view.) It is the failure of the leisured to achieve practical
ends which the business mind objects to. What is potentially
truly objectionable in the leisured attitude, however, is the false
relation to the rest of the world which it can share with the
business attitude.

If money as a means rather than an end is a horror to the
world which is making it—the symbol of unspeakable potentialities and the efficient cause of pernicious effects—it is something
else to those who have it, have it perhaps through the efforts
of their business-minded forbears but are able anyway to see its
potentialities from the inside. For Henry James, Sr., the fortune
which he had, with effort, inherited from his father was the
means whereby his children would be liberated from the need
to make money and hence from the worldly sense of success,
the business imagination; and whereby they would be free to
cultivate that other imagination, the fruit of which was to be
that social virtue which the father valued above all else. Indeed,
the elder James was determined, as Le Clair says, "to spare not

a dollar to secure for his children absolute freedom from mercenary motives and to provide for them that atmosphere . . . in which they would develop into upright men, men in whom goodness was induced by their natural sympathy toward it."[7]

It was the paternal fortune which permitted the trips back and forth to Europe, in which the future novelist discovered in old castles, museums, and pensions a sense of history, of art, and perhaps of America; the strangely Proustian theatrical excursions; and the seemingly chaotic system of education which involved tours of duty at assorted obscure Swiss schools and the (for the young James) mysterious comings and goings of various tutors and governesses—in short, those conditions which allowed the young boy most fully to "observe" and to "gape," to cultivate the sensibility of one "on whom nothing is lost." It is a tantalizing question whether a Henry James deprived of the opportunities for observation given him by the family fortune (the family fortune, of course, not a little assisted by the family sensibility) would have retained his susceptibility to impressions, would have found as much to "bristle" in an acquisitive environment as in one of leisure, whether a family environment dedicated to those pursuits of which the James inheritance relieved him would have blunted the incredibly fine instrument which was his mind. A Henry James out of the Jamesian context seems unthinkable, but that is perhaps because it is only in his context that we do have him. Nevertheless, it seems obvious that the background which the family wealth provided him allowed the observational and imaginative powers of the young James to operate at maximal intensity and to register that sense of life which he would later convert into art.

Yet James's attitude toward money was ever a complex one. If he saw it as the source of a potentially unlimited experience, he also saw it, or the need for it, as a limit placed on the potential of the imagination. His sense of the leisured life's possibilities and his personal generosity,[8] a generosity which found a precursor and a great example in that of his parents, were so curiously commingled even in his later life with an anxiety regarding money[9] that we find Edith Wharton, a frequent dinner guest at Lamb House during James's final years, observing that

> an anxious frugality was combined with the wish that the usually solitary guest (there were never at most more than two at a time) should not suffer too greatly from the contrast between his or her supposed habits of luxury and the privations imposed by the host's conviction that he was on the brink of ruin. If anyone in a pecuniary difficulty appealed to James for help he gave it without counting; but in his daily life he was haunted by the spectre of impoverishment.[10]

Throughout his life a tension obtained in the mind of the great novelist between his sense of money as the source of potential imaginative experience and his sense of it as the mere hard cash by which one had to live. That tension carried over into his fiction as the metaphor for an even greater tension, the dilemma of the imagination in its encounter with the world.

An examination of cash and its conversion into the stuff of consciousness in the fiction of Henry James must necessarily be a selective one. Dietrichson has amply demonstrated the all-prevalance of money in James's work,[11] and to indicate how it operates in each individual work in which it functions significantly would require an examination of several volumes' length. The procedure adopted, therefore, has been to consider those early tales and novels in which the potential implications of the financial motif are most successfully, or at least most tantalizingly, adumbrated; to continue with an examination of *The Portrait of a Lady*, the first of James's novels in which the fact of money is the nexus of meaning, the "key to it all"; and to conclude with a reading of *The Golden Bowl*, that Jamesian *summa* in which the metaphorical language of money becomes the vessel of the dialectic. A coda on *The Ivory Tower* will indicate James's inverting therein the implications and the mode of *The Golden Bowl*. Such a treatment excludes even so obviously germane a work as *The Wings of the Dove*, but the purpose is neither to be comprehensive nor to provide anything like an

economic theory of Henry James. Rather, it is to illuminate
certain key texts by analyzing what is the central Jamesian
metaphor for the central Jamesian theme, the relation of the
self to that which is "other."

CHAPTER TWO

The Early Tales

> I was charmed with my idea, which would take, however, much
> working out; and precisely because it had so much to give, I think,
> must I have dropped it for this time into the deep well of uncon-
> scious cerebration: not without the hope, doubtless, that it might
> eventually emerge from that reservoir, as one had already known
> the buried treasure to come to light, with a firm iridescent surface
> and a notable increase of weight.
>
> — from the preface to *The American*

THE financial motif is absent, in any significant form, from
"The Story of a Year," the first published fiction to bear the
name of Henry James.[1] The absence is anything but indicative
of what was to follow, for well over half the short stories and
all the novels written before *The Portrait of a Lady* involve the
financial motif in some form—if not in a central position, at least
in a peripheral one. All the prominent Jamesian themes, from
the artist's dilemma to the "Sacred Fount" relationship, exist in
at least nascent form in the early short stories; and if their inter-
relationship is not so organic as in the later work, the reason is
simply James's less than complete grasp of the possibilities for
interpenetration and mutual illumination inherent in the materials most attractive to his imagination. In short, the reason is
his artistic youth. One can with relative ease talk about money
in "A Landscape Painter," where its function, if central, is
rather straightforward and separable, whereas talking about
money in *The Golden Bowl*, to take the most extreme example,
virtually entails talking about everything else in the novel too.

Money is inescapably there in the early stories. Locksley,

the title figure of "A Landscape Painter," has a hundred thousand a year, and Adela in "A Day of Days" a "very pretty little fortune" (*LP*, 15, 178). Gertrude, the heroine of "Poor Richard," is "massive in person, and rich besides" (*LP*, 72), a sort of proto-Rosanna Gaw. The central character of "The Story of a Masterpiece" is a "good natured millionaire" (*EUT*, 119). Ambrose Tester of "The Path of Duty" has "property worth some twenty thousand a year" (*SR* I:146), and the title character of "Benvolio" "the voice as it were of a man whose fortune has been made for him, and who assumes, a trifle egotistically, that the rest of the world is equally at leisure to share with him the sweets of life, to pluck the wayside flowers, and chase the butterflies afield" (*MF*, 344–345). "A Passionate Pilgrim" turns on the question of ancestral property; "A Light Man" on the struggle for an inheritance. Max, the cynical and mercenary narrator of the latter (he describes his own career as "So-and-So's Progress to a Mercenary Marriage"), who is guilefully attempting to direct the inheritance of the dying Mr. Sloane from his friend Theodore to himself, says of his potential benefactor that he "wraps himself in his money as in a wadded dressing gown, and goes trundling through life on his little gold wheels, as warm and close as an unweaned baby" (*ME*, 167, 170). The Colonel in "Professor Fargo" is financially dependent upon the charlatan Professor, who eventually seduces his daughter away from him. In "Georgina's Reasons" Milly Theory, the Ur-Milly Theale, urging her sister Kate (who shares nothing with Kate Croy but name) to marry the man she herself loves after her death, says, "When I am gone there will be plenty for both of you"; and later in the story it is observed of her brother's vacuous wife's circle that "the stamp of money was on all their thoughts and doings" (*SR*, I:329, 337).

Throughout the early short stories money abounds; and though the financial motif is often less than integral to the story, its fundamental interest attends those relations into which it enters and the attitudes among the characters which it engenders. One fairly obvious example occurs in "A Light Man," the narrator of which, Max, surely the least subtle of James's first-person villains, is a completely acquisitive being,[2] interested only in the cash fact of money as an end in itself. Contrasted with his attitude toward money is the somewhat obscure one of his friend and financial rival, Theodore, who protests to him at the end:

> "I *did* value my prospects of coming into Mr. Sloane's property. I valued them for my poor sister's sake, as well as for my own, so long as they were the natural reward of conscientious service, and not the prize of hypocrisy and cunning. With another man than you I never would have contested such a prize. But I loved you, even as my rival. You played with me, deceived me, betrayed me. I held my ground, hoping and longing to purge you of your error by the touch of your old pledges of affection."

Max replies:

> "You say you loved me. If so, you ought to love me still. It wasn't for my virtue; for I never had any, or pretended to any. In anything I have done recently, therefore, there has been no inconsistency. I never pretended to love you. I don't understand the word, in the sense you attach to it. I don't understand the feeling, between men. To me, love means quite another thing. You give it a meaning of your own; you enjoy the profit of your invention; it's no more than just that you should pay the penalty." (*ME*, 198–199)

Theodore's reasoning is rather opaque, and the hint of inversion here, supported by the rest of the story, decidedly complicates the issue. Still, it seems obvious that Max does not "understand the feeling" at all, that the other "thing" which love means for him is, at best, judging by his conduct and by the handy title which he provides for his own life, a combination of lust and financial gain. No more than Mr. Sloane has he "known any but mercenary affection" (*ME*, 174), though in his case the criticism applies to affection *for* rather than *from* others. Max's incomprehension of Theodore even expresses itself in the terms of financial deals: "enjoy the profit," "pay the penalty." His argument is that one is not reproachable so long as his actions are not inconsistent with what he claims for himself, that one can be held accountable for his actions only if he himself proclaims them virtuous. This specious logic and its attendant acquisitiveness are opposed by the more complex (as presented, if not as done) attitude of Theodore, whose acquisitiveness expresses itself as duty and reward ("conscientious service"), charity (toward his sister) and love.[3]

The title character of "Master Eustace" is not unlike Max in his cynicism, charm, and complete egotism. Having been born to an adequate fortune, however, he is not mercenary, and his avaricious and aggrandizing impulses manifest themselves in a more complex form. Thoroughly spoiled in his childhood by his mother, whose personal frugality was inspired by a desire to deny her children nothing, he has "had a particular fancy for the moon—for everything bright and inaccessible and absurd" (ME, 12). He is imaginative, but his is the imagination of possession. "Eustace has no head for money matters," says his mother, "he only knows how to spend"; but his governess sees him with a somewhat more objective eye: "He talked a great deal of his property, and, though he had a great aversion to figures, he knew the amount of his expectations before he was out of jackets" (ME, 37, 24). He combines a cash-register mind with a self-indulgent prodigality. Money is a peripheral matter in this story, but Eustace's attitude toward it is indicative of that possessiveness which motivates, at the end, his fatal denunciation of his mother for having remarried (the man who proves to be his actual father)—an act which is for him neglect and betrayal, but which is for her both the renewal of love and the chance to provide her son with the affection of his true father. Eustace's blindness to his mother's devotion, a devotion which can be seen as in large measure responsible for that blindness, is a denial of her autonomy—an attitude placing her among the items of his property.

"Guest's Confession" is a good deal more financially oriented. It even features two members of that race comparatively rare in James, the businessman, engaged in the "downtown" activities of making deals, embezzling and the like. One of these, Edgar Musgrave, is an eminently objectionable sort, the archetypal shrewd businessman, whose credo is: "I hate to see money bring in less than it may. My imagination loves a good investment. I respect my property, I respect other people's" (TC, 166)—and who is capable of exclaiming on his death-bed, "I might have got better, and richer" (TC, 210). This quintessence of the business imagination is opposed by Guest, an aging and seedily dandyish businessman, whose interest lies less in playing with the intricacies of the market than in being a "gentleman" and providing his daughter with money, which he insists she should spend lavishly. He is not cut out for the business role, as his daughter observes: "All the business in the world, for a man of his open, joyous temper, doesn't pay for an hour's depression. I can't bear to sit by and see him embittered and spoiled by this muddle of stocks and shares. . . . We are quite rich enough, and we need nothing more. He tries to persuade me that I have expensive tastes, but I've never spent money but to please him" (TC, 193).

Guest is much more suited to the role occupied by the narrator of the story, Edgar's stepbrother David, whose patrimony, double that of Edgar, enables him to live the life of the man of the world and to indulge (with, he assures us, the bulk of his inheritance) his taste for clothes. Indeed, the similarity between Guest and the narrator, in looks and in temperament, is one of the main points of the story and the one around which most of its ironies revolve. Suggested in the description and the action, it is made overt by Laura Guest's saying to David: "And I think, too, that I speak to you of my father with peculiar freedom, because—because, somehow, you remind me of him. . . . You are genial, and gentle, and essentially honest, like him; and like him, you're addicted to saying a little more than it would be fair to expect you to stand to" (TC, 193–194).

At the periphery of the story (it is one of James's more expansive and highly populated early efforts) and completing the financial design are Mrs. Beck, with whom Guest is in love, and Mr. Crawford, her "cousin." Mrs. Beck is notable for the

Arcadian quality of her physical preservation, but, as the narrator observes, "[her] morality was not Arcadian; or if it was, it was that of a shepherdess with a keen eye to the state of the wool and the mutton market, and a lively perception of the possible advantages of judicious partnership" (*TC*, 186). She is plainly on the make, though her preference for Crawford's millions is tempered by a militant aesthetic sense which balks at his roughness and inclines toward Guest's "distinction" (*TC*, 196). True to her dominant trait, however, she deserts Guest when his financial ruin becomes apparent, and is last seen brewing tea for the thoroughly infatuated Crawford.[4]

Crawford is the stereotypic self-made millionaire from the West—he owns a silver mine in Arizona—sprawling, modest, thoroughly honest and open. He could be described as the prototype of Newman in *The American* were he not so broadly drawn (though the humor at his expense is not different in kind from that at Newman's) and were his taste in women not so execrable (Mrs. Beck being obviously closer kin to Mrs. Headway in "The Siege of London" than to Claire de Cintré). Such touches as "that Arizonian tinkle which served with him as the prelude to renewed utterance" (*TC*, 188)—a rather less alluring and more sinister forerunner of Daisy Buchanan's famous voice —render him little more than a type done in a series of gestures, whereas Newman will be an attempt to provide a consciousness for the gestures.

The action of the story, briefly, concerns Guest's cheating Edgar in a business deal (the details are characteristically murky) and Edgar's retribution in forcing him to write a confession which will be made public unless the funds are restored. David, who, before learning of the fraud, has become attracted to Guest's daughter, is witness to the humiliating scene in which Guest is made to confess and beg for Edgar's forgiveness on his knees. Edgar, even after Guest's reparation, continues to exact his vengeance by not returning the confession to Guest, but at his death the damning paper passes into the hands of his stepbrother.

The rest of the story is concerned with David's attempts

to marry Laura, to manipulate Guest into permitting his daughter to marry the man who was present at his humiliation and who took no steps to prevent it. The balance at the end is handled with some subtlety. David offers to place his funds at Guest's disposal, but Guest, outraged, not inaccurately interprets the gesture as an attempt to buy him off and furiously rejects David's money and his suit for Laura's hand. David—who foreshadows those Jamesian narrators and centers of consciousness, such as those of The Sacred Fount and "The Liar," toward whom the irony of the story is directed (although much of the criticism of David is explicit and even recognized by himself)—piqued at Guest's obstinacy, attempts to force his hand with threats of revealing the confession to Laura. Conscience, however, at length compels him to burn the evidence in the presence of Guest and Laura, a gesture which breaks down Guest's last defenses, already largely shattered by Mrs. Beck's refusal.

The circumstances at the end are rather like those of The American, but there are significant differences, the most obvious being that "Guest's Confession" ends "happily." More important, however, is the contrast between the David-Guest relation and the Newman-Bellegarde one. In The American the emphasis falls on the disparity in quality of mind between Newman and the Bellegardes. The Bellegardes, seeing Newman whole if unable to comprehend him, know that he will be incapable of carrying through his threat. Guest, on the other hand, does not doubt for a minute that David will carry through his, and it is this certainty which causes his agonized inaction. He himself has been capable of fraud, and he sees David in his own terms, which the young narrator to an extent merits. The similarity between Guest and the narrator has been observed—a similarity which manifests itself most strongly in their dandyism, their devotion to their external appearance. The narrator is able in the confession scene to lessen the severity of Edgar's vengeance, but his desire not to be involved in such a sordid business gives some justice to Guest's charge of cowardice, for

David here manifests a weakness not unlike that which permitted Guest so easily to commit fraud.

Indeed, it is not so much his guilty action which torments Guest throughout the story (though he admits to being unable to confront his daughter on the day of its commission) as his loss of face, the destruction of the external appearance which he presents to the world. He hates David less because the young man has not intervened than because he has seen him grovel. It is under the external form of the man of the world that Guest defends his action to Edgar: "I would have rearranged matters. It was just a temporary convenience. I supposed I was dealing with a man of common courtesy. But what are you to say to a gentleman who says, 'Sir, I trust you,' and then looks through the keyhole?" (TC, 173). The irony is all too obvious, and yet, in the light of Edgar's inflexibility, Guest's weakness is almost appealing. He has acted for his daughter, even though he misconstrues completely what she wants, and he is concerned with his honor, though he confuses it with his appearance in the eyes of others.

The justice of Edgar's claims against Guest is undeniable; but the justice of his pronouncing them is denied thoroughly by the fundamental confusion at the base of everything he says, a confusion most apparent in his statement that "a man's property, sir, is a man's person" (TC, 175). He is so completely the man of business that he has lost his identity in his possessions. He is, in fact, little more than his own bank account. "He was a man of conscience," says David. "He made honesty something unlovely, but he was rigidly honest. He demanded simply his dues, and he collected them to the last farthing" (TC, 164). His conscience cannot extend beyond the matter of paying debts, and even there it is most concerned with debts owed him. "Honesty" in such a context is a nearly meaningless term, and, even in this connection of upholding a contract, Edgar behaves dishonestly in not returning the confession to Guest after the reparation. Some hints of conscience seem to show in Edgar's death-bed delirium, but they are little more than vestigial, to be associated, probably, with the psychological reasons for the way he is rather than with his mind as it is given. It is questionable whether a mind so limited, a self so completely merged with its possessions, can even be regarded as a moral agent. (The question, in a somewhat different form, is equally raised by Gilbert Osmond in *The Portrait of a Lady*.) If not, the case of Edgar at least stands as a black and inhuman backdrop against which the ironic little moral drama of Guest and David, with its nice mutations of honesty and honor, is played.

If Edgar has no identity outside his possessions, Gertrude Whittaker, the heroine of "Poor Richard," is aware that her identity may be smothered by her property.[5] Three suitors vie for Gertrude's hand—Captain Severn, whom she loves and who loves her, but who will not declare his love until he has sufficient money of his own to repudiate the implication that he is marrying her for hers; Major Luttrel, who is not in love with her but simply wants her money; and Richard Clare, a poor but ardent young farmer, who is in love with her and does not hesitate to declare the fact. Severn is deterred from pressing his suit by a fear that the world will see him as mercenary. Not so Richard. One is informed that "it was assumed without question that the necessity of raising money was the mainspring of Richard's suit. It is needless to inform the reader that this assumption was . . . without a leg to stand upon. Our hero had faults enough, but to be mercenary was not one of them" (*LP*, 87). Luttrel is like Edgar in his exclusive concern with money, Severn rather like Guest in his concern with an external image of himself; but Richard is interested only in the relation between Gertrude and himself. Neither Gertrude's money nor the world's opinion matters to him.

Gertrude, however, realizes toward the end that her money has mattered in determining her relations: "A vague suspicion that her money had done her an incurable wrong inspired her with a profound distaste for the care of it. She felt cruelly hedged out from human sympathy by her bristling possessions. 'If I had had five hundred dollars a year,' she said in a frequent parenthesis, 'I might have pleased him' [Severn]." And later: "I'm a mere mass of possessions: what I am, is nothing to what I have" (LP, 147, 154). She sees herself as dwarfed by—and if for herself independent of, for others identical with—her possessions. At the end she comes to love Richard, the only one whose love for her "self" has been unqualified by her possessions. He, however, by the operation of a corollary of what John Bayley calls "Proust's Law"[6] (in this case, that A never loves B until B has ceased loving A), is no longer in love with her, having through his love for her discovered the nature of his own self (which discovery is rather Proustian too); and Gertrude, having gone to Europe, is finally viewed taking refuge, ironically, behind what she has deplored as destructive to her relationships: "Her great wealth, of which she was wont to complain that it excluded her from human sympathy, now affords her a most efficient protection" (LP, 174).

Locksley, the title character in James's third story, "A Landscape Painter," is also afflicted with an enormous fortune which he wishes to escape. He has just broken his engagement, and, as the narrator says, the explanation "most popular with Locksley's well-wishers was that he had backed out . . . only on flagrant evidence of the lady's—what, faithlessness?—on overwhelming proof of the most mercenary spirit on the part of Miss Leary" (LP, 8). Locksley declares (the bulk of the story is in the form of his diary) his belief in the independence of his identity from his wealth and determines to be valued only for himself, "to abjure for a while my conventional self, and to assume a simple, natural character. How can a man be simple and natural who is known to have a hundred thousand a year? That is the supreme curse. It's bad enough to have it: to be known to have it, to be known only because you have it, is most damnable . . . . I have determined to stand upon my own merits" (LP, 15–16). The difficulties he will face, however, are evident in the language he uses. He will throw off his "conventional self," the role which his money forces him to play, and "assume a simple, natural character." But if that character has to be assumed, it is not his own, nor are the merits on which he is then to be judged. In short, his "conventional self" may be a function of his money, but it is still his "self."

The story bears out what is implicit in his words. Locksley goes to the seashore and takes up residence with the Blunts, the Captain and his daughter Esther, for both of whom, the father confides, "money's an object" (*LP*, 17). He is soon in love with the girl, and his proposal of marriage is accepted. At the end of the story, his revelation of his wealth to his bride is met by her acknowledgment that she is aware of it, that she has taken advantage of his recent illness to read his diary and discover the fact, and that she is marrying him because of it:

> "You intimated in one place in your book that I am born for wealth and splendor. I believe I am. You pretend to hate your money; but you would not have had me without it. If you really love me,—and I think you do,—you will not let this make any difference. . . . I never said I loved you. I never deceived you in that. I said I would be your wife. So I will, faithfully. I haven't so much heart as you think; and yet, too, I have a great deal more. I am incapable of more than one deception." (*LP*, 65–66)

Though brutal, Esther's speech accurately indicates that Locksley's romantic notion of an independent self is unrealizable. She has been prompted to read the diary by her sense of the disparity between what Locksley represents himself to be and what he really is, and her intuition supports Fitzgerald's position, in the famous exchange with Hemingway, that the rich are different from other people, and not only because they have more money. Locksley's self is not independent of its external conditions; it exists only in relation to them. In denying them, he denies his own identity. At the very end of the story he charges Esther with "the act of a false woman," and she counters: "A false woman? No,—simply of a woman. I am a woman, sir. . . . Come, you be a man!" (*LP*, 67). His position has been as false as hers; each of them has been capable of one, though only one, deception.

Still, Esther's vigorously triumphant conclusion rings a little hollow, if only in its rather disheartening implication that all women marry for money. For, although Locksley cannot be said to exist independent of his externals, it is seemingly with the externals alone that Esther is concerned.[7] Locksley should have been forewarned by her apparent straightforwardness in an earlier skirmish. When he asserts that he "can't afford" to marry, she replies:

> "Marry a rich woman."
> I shook my head.
> "Why not?" asked Miss Blunt. "Because people would accuse you of being mercenary? What of that? I mean to marry the first rich man who offers. Do you know that I am tired of living alone in this weary old way, teaching little girls their gamut, and turning and patching my dresses? I mean to marry the first man who offers."
> "Even if he is poor?"
> "Even if he is poor, ugly, and stupid." (LP, 39–40)

Miss Blunt's bluntness is quite studied and, as the ending of the story shows, not entirely accurate. But her concern with money and her desire to alter her position are explicit in the Captain's narrative to Locksley of her first engagement. She has told her father that she will marry her fiancé only "when John grows rich enough." The engagement is broken after a year, John evidently never having attained the requisite bracket; later she learns that, ironically, he "is accumulating money very fast in the China trade" (LP, 43–44). Esther's faith in externals is again emphasized when, to a compliment on her looks from Locksley, she replies, "But it's not I; it's the accessories" (LP, 51). Finally, in a recollection of their first meeting, Locksley urges, "You told me you remembered the occasion in question perfectly," and Esther answers: "I meant the circumstances. I remember what we had for tea; I remember what dress I wore. But I don't remember my feelings. They were naturally not very memorable" (LP, 58). It is more than likely that she is dissimulating; she was probably thinking of marriage when she first met him, and if so, that fact does not slip her now. But the nature of her language locates her major preoccupation with the external.

"A Landscape Painter" implies, then, through the device of Locksley's wealth, the necessary connection between the self and its external conditions. It does not, however, imply that the self is nothing more than those external conditions. Esther's words, in what they deny, imply the opposite of her position— namely, that an occasion possesses a texture of feeling and thought as well as a material texture. The story is significant, not as a particularly satisfactory piece of work itself, but as an extremely early treatment of the problem of internal relation— a problem, frequently handled in terms of money, which is central to James's later and more than satisfactory work.

"Longstaff's Marriage," dating from 1878, suggests a sense of money different from those we have been considering. Longstaff, dying of consumption, falls in love with Diana Belfield, whom he sees daily on the beach but does not know. As a dying request, he eventually asks her to make the gesture of marrying him: "It will enable me to do something for you—the only thing I can do. I have property,—lands, houses, a great many beautiful things,—things I have loved, and am very sorry to be leaving behind me. . . . It can only give you a larger liberty" (*ME*, 86–87). The blow to his pride offered by her refusal restores his health, but she, discovering later that she loves him, wastes away, and finally, immediately before her death, obtains from him, though he no longer loves her, that gesture which she had denied him. It is another "Proust's Law" story, but its protagonists are much closer to Isabel Archer and Ralph Touchett[8] than to Gertrude Whittaker and Richard Clare. Diana, like Isabel, cherishes her independence and does not wish to marry; Longstaff, like Ralph, wishes to bequeath her, as a gesture of unselfish love, the money which will be the means to "a larger liberty." Money figures here prophetically, if not very fully, as the expression of magnanimity, the condition of personal freedom, and the symbol of human potentiality.

CHAPTER THREE

The Early Novels

THE six early novels all offer ample documentation of Jame's interest in what we have called—for want of a better term to signify the full range of connection into which money and its associated concepts enter—the "financial motif." None of these novels need detain us inordinately long, and two of them, *Washington Square*, because it is extremely familiar and because its treatment of money is stunningly straightforward, and *Confidence*, because, though glistening on the surface with all the most important Jamesian themes, it does nothing very comprehensible with any of them, we shall neglect entirely.

I

Watch and Ward, James's early and rightly orphaned first novel (the honor of "first novel" always fell to *Roderick Hudson* in James's mention), presents three suitors for the hand of the orphaned girl Nora. One is the wealthy Roger Lawrence, who has adopted Nora as a child and has brought her up with the intention of marrying her when she reaches the right age. At the beginning of the story, Nora's father has committed suicide after Roger, whom he had encountered by chance in the reading room of a hotel, refused him the hundred dollars which would have relieved him of financial pressures. Roger has, rather feebly, considering the size of Jamesian bank accounts, offered him ten dollars, and his discovery of the suicide prompts him to say, with apparent lack of authorial irony: "It gives me a sickening sense of connexion with this bloodshed. But how could I

help it? All the same, I wish he had taken my ten dollars"
(WW, 14). We have already been warned that Roger "of
course had no imagination" (WW, 7), but the failure of imagination here, as in many spots throughout the book, seems to be
in part James's. In any case, Roger decides to adopt the dead
man's child, after considering her as a gamble: "Should he sub-
scribe the whole sum, in the name of human charity? He
thought of the risk. She was an unknown quantity. Her nature,
her heritage, her good and bad possibilities, were an unsolved
problem." Later he informs the girl, referring to his desire to
marry her, that he expects a return for his investment: "Nora,
Nora, these are not vulgar alms; I expect a return. One of these
days you must pay your debt" (WW, 18, 42); and the matter
of the "debt," particularly Nora's consciousness of it, looms
large throughout the novel.

If the financial aspect of Roger's attitude is essentially
metaphorical, it is otherwise with the remaining suitors. One is
Roger's cousin Hubert, a clergyman decidedly of this world,
whose "observation was exercised rather less in the interest of
general truth than of particular profit" (WW, 31). Hubert
envisages himself as a man of imagination, though there is little
evidence apart from his own testimony: "There are men born
to imagine things, others born to do them. Evidently I am not
one of the doers. But I imagine things, I assure you!" The scene
is that of his proposal to Nora, and the image which he chooses
to depict her as the fulfilment of his nature is significant: "I
am like a purse filled at one end with small coin and empty at
the other. Perhaps the other will never know the golden rattle!"
(WW, 131). His imagination is cash-oriented, as his final encounter with Nora attests. She, alone and destitute in New
York, has come to Hubert for help and has divined his reluc-
tance to be the support she needs. Discovering the right way to
let him off (it is the most characteristically Jamesian passage in
the novel), she translates her appeal for aid into an appeal for
money. "Money? Would money buy his release? He took out

his purse and grasped a roll of bills; then suddenly he was overwhelmed by a sense of his cruelty" (WW, 191). He senses what his own imagination has been.

The third suitor, Fenton, makes no claims to imagination. He is the man of action—"He had an irresistible air of action, alertness, and purpose" (WW, 60), and an inhabitant of the territory of "doing"—"In the West you can do something!" (WW, 63). "Doing," however, is for Fenton an extremely simple concept: it means merely getting money. In his suit "Nora was but the means; Roger's presumptive wealth and bounty were the end." He intimates that "he was incapable of any other relation to a fact than a desire to turn it to pecuniary account" (WW 58). Even Fenton's office reflects for Nora the essence of his attitude: "But the desk, the stove, the iron safe, the chairs, the sordid ink-spotted walls, were as blank and impersonal as so many columns of figures" (WW, 160).

More suggestive than these fairly straightforward characterizations is James's treatment of Nora. She is seen as a Princess (WW, 44) and as a creature of possibilities which are threatened by Hubert ("Hubert's words had potently foreshadowed the forfeiture of sweet possibilities") but realizable through the experience of Europe[1] and an infinite bank account (WW, 84, 90, 111). The hint of future Jamesian developments is obvious. Also, she is a "performer" whom the wealthy and managerial Mrs. Keith puts through her paces (WW, 124), much as Mrs. Lowder will Kate Croy in *The Wings of the Dove* and Mrs. Assingham Maggie Verver in *The Golden Bowl*. After Roger's proposal, Nora tends to take in cash terms what Roger has meant as a granted freedom but what his insistence on "debt" has left quite open to her misinterpretation: "Why, when he took her, had he not drawn up his terms and made his bargain? She would have kept the bargain to the letter; she would have taught herself to be his wife. Duty then would have been duty; sentiment would have been sentiment" (WW, 155). Duty as motive, however, eventually disappears, and sentiment is finally recognized after the exposure of Fenton and Hubert. The sensitive gentleman rather unaccountably gets the girl, and the potential complexities of the financial motif remain unrealized.

II

Roderick Hudson, despite its obvious flaws, represents a remarkable five years' advance over *Watch and Ward.* We hear a good deal less about money than in the earlier novel, but what we do hear is much more integrated and, hence, much more significant. The theme receives essentially two major developments in the course of the novel. The first concerns both the attitude of Christina Light's mother toward her and Christina's own sense of herself. The second concerns the relation between Rowland Mallet's money and Roderick Hudson's genius and, concomitantly, the relation between the will and the imagination. Both developments are thus concerned with concepts of the self and its relations. As the former is similar to treatments which we have discussed earlier, we shall turn to it first.

Christina Light's "education" has been directed solely to the end of her marrying fabulously. Her mother, devoting herself entirely to the achievement of her daughter's success, which will be, in effect, recompense for the success she herself has missed, the beauty she has lost, capitalizes on the girl's astounding beauty ("I've raised money on that girl's face!" she tells Rowland; "I've taken her to the Jews and bidden her put off her veil and let down her hair, show her teeth, her shoulders, her arms, all sorts of things, and asked if the mother of that young lady was n't safe!"), and she sees her own fulfillment in selling her daughter: "She considered that she had been performing a pious duty in bringing up Christina to carry herself, 'marked' very high and in the largest letters, to market" (NY, I:252, 249). Consequently, Christina's sense of herself as a marketable commodity is strong—James intensifies it considerably in the New York Edition (the "market" image, for example, does not appear in the 1876 edition)—and her sense of her mother bitter. During her first scene in Roderick's studio, she says to her mother of the bust which he proposes to do of her, "You can always sell it" (RH, 144); in the revised version, James expands this to "You can always get something for it. . . . You always get something for everything. I dare say that with patience you'll still get something even for me" (NY, I:158).

Christina's sense of herself as an object for others, in fact, is so strong that she has little sense of her own identity, and her capriciousness and dramatic posturings are attempts to actualize the possibilities of a self in which she can believe. As her own history is just the history of what her mother has made of her, the histories which she invents for herself are equally real:

> She had a fictitious history in which she believed much more fondly than in her real one, and an infinite capacity for extemporised reminiscence adapted to the mood of the hour. She liked to carry herself further and further, to see herself in situation and action; and the vivacity and spontaneity of her character gave her really a starting-point in experience, so that the many-coloured flowers of fiction that blossomed in her talk were perversions of fact only if one could n't take them for sincerities of spirit. And Rowland felt that whatever she said of herself might have been, under the imagined circumstances. (NY, I:278–279)

Christina has been designed to conquer the world and her attraction to the world is strong, but she cherishes the notion of a "higher self" (NY, I:407) for which she is willing to renounce the world and Prince Casamassima's money. Her sense of herself is so unsure, however, her "higher self" so much an abstraction which she wants to live up to, that she needs to concretize her "self" in a totally unexpected action which she can measure by the standards of others. As Madame Grandoni says of her (though not in the New York Edition): "She needs to think well of herself; she knows a fine character, easily, when she meets one; she hates to suffer by comparison, even though the comparison is made by herself alone; and when the estimate she may have made of herself grows vague, she needs to do something to give it definite, impressive form" (*RH*, 337). When Rowland asks her to give up Roderick, she questions him: "But tell me, shall you consider—admitting your proposition—that in ceasing to be nice to Mr. Hudson, so that he may go about his business, I do something magnanimous, heroic, sublime, something with a fine name like that?" (NY, I:288).

Her "higher self" has to be defined for her. In desiring to do something "fine," she wills as an end less the act itself to which the name applies than the application of the name to the act. Her "higher self," in short, is a role which she will assume providing she is applauded for it. It is essentially imitative, and her renunciation of the Prince takes the form of not doing something Mary Garland would not do. After her hand has been forced, she acknowledges as much to Rowland: "I think I've given up trying to imitate Miss Garland." But she still cherishes the memory of her "higher self," whether it was in fact hers or not: "What does it matter whether I was insincere or not? I can't conceive of anything mattering less. I was very fine—is n't it true?" (NY, I:489, 491). Christina's submission to the world is an acknowledgement that she sees her "higher self" as a gesture of renunciation made before the world, a gesture which would be invalidated were the rupture to come from the Prince and not her.

One may, in all of this, seem to be shortchanging Christina, who is without doubt the most interesting, vital, and multifaceted character in the novel. Certainly Rowland's sense of her magnanimity is great, and his Puritan consciousness is strongly enough drawn to make us accord his appraisal considerable weight. Christina has the potentiality and the ability to create the great forms to which she aspires; but her lack of understanding of them, a lack almost necessitated by the forms which the world and her proprietor-mother have imposed upon her nebulous self, will not allow her to live into them. "Well, she has done what she was to do," says Madame Grandoni. "She was nobly to decline it—yet not to miss it" (NY, I:420). Yet this surface reconcilation of the self and the world has been less her fate than what shortly before Rowland saw for her: "Christina, meanwhile, had really for the time been soaring aloft, to his vision, and though in such flights of her moral nature—the energy of which now affected him as real—there was a certain painful effort and tension of wing, it was none the less piteous to imagine her being rudely jerked down to base earth" (NY, I:410). The wings of her possibility are pulled into the world— they will flap vainly in *The Princess Casamassima*—but she prefigures, strangely, the rather different descent into the world, and its effect thereon, of the later Jamesian dove.

Money and the world are one for Christina Light; but for Roderick Hudson Christina is the world and money a kind of surrogate self, the condition for realizing the potentiality of his genius. It is Rowland Mallet's money which is to permit Roderick to go to Europe and there maximize his artistic powers. Rowland himself, in providing the money for and supervising Roderick's European experience, is, as it were, letting Roderick perform his creative role for him. "Do you know," he says to his cousin, "I sometimes think that I'm a man of genius half-finished? The genius has been left out, the faculty of expression is wanting; but the need for expression remains" (NY, I:8). Roderick provides the genius. "I can't do such things myself," Rowland says later, "but when I see a young man of genius standing helpless and hopeless for want of capital, I feel—and it's no affectation of humility, I assure you—as if it would give at least a reflected usefulness to my own life to offer him his opportunity" (NY, I:49). He has seen "true happiness" as "getting out of one's self"; and get out of himself he does, to the extent that he is soon "living Roderick's intellectual life ... as well as his own" (NY, I:7, 88–89).

Roderick has, before Rowland's offer, lain in his innocent American valley and looked "away to the blue distances, the 'purple rim' of the poet, which had the wealth of the world, all the unattainable of life, beyond them" (NY, I:72)—a passage which James, significantly, added in the New York Edition.

Perhaps even more significantly, it is closely related to his concept of the "romantic" as given in the preface to the New York Edition of *The American*: "The romantic stands, on the other hand, for the things that, with all the facilities in the world, all the wealth and all the courage and all the wit and all the adventure, we never *can* directly know; the things that can reach us only through the beautiful circuit and subterfuge of our thought and our desire" (NY, II:xvi).

Roderick's vision is romantic—it is the wealth of his own imagination which he truly seeks and which he loses in attaining the wealth of the world. His romanticism is evident in his rather ridiculous prattle about his art: "I mean to do things that will be simple and vast and infinite" (*RH*, 107). Abstraction and nondifferentiation characterize his idea of his art: "They shall be simply divine forms. They shall be Beauty; they shall be Wisdom; they shall be Power; they shall be Genius; they shall be Daring. . . . I mean to do the Morning; I mean to do the Night! I mean to do the Ocean and the Mountains, the Moon and the West Wind. I mean to make a magnificent image of my Native Land" (NY, I:118).

Roderick's genius, as evinced in his early statue of a young man drinking, is associated with the ludicrous figure of the sculptor Herr Schafgans as described by Madame Grandoni: "He never painted anything so profane as a man taking a drink, but his figures were all of the simple and slender and angular pattern, and nothing if not innocent—like this one of yours" (*RH*, 110). Other points are emphasized in the New York Edition elaboration of the passage: "He never painted anything so profane as a man taking a drink, for none of his people had anything so vulgar as an appetite. They were all angles and edges—they looked like diagrams of human nature. They were figures if you please, but geometrical figures." (NY, I:120). Herr Schafgans is, of course, a parody of Roderick—he falls in love with a coarse Roman model and goes completely to seed—but the association of abstraction, angularity and innocence is highly significant in respect to Roderick's art, for when the innocence goes, so do the other qualities, and so in effect, does Roderick's genius.

All of Roderick Hudson's successful productions, with one outstanding exception, are characterized by the innocence of the American romantic vision. We have noted Madame Grandoni's comment on the innocence of Roderick's first masterpiece, the statue, completed in America, of the youth drinking from the cup, and Roderick himself grandly points out the significance of that work: "Why, he's youth, you know; he's innocence, he's health, he's strength, he's curiosity. . . . The cup is knowledge, pleasure, experience. Anything of that kind" (NY, I:27). Its larger significance, of course, is that it prefigures the movement of the entire novel, and it is a nice paradox that Roderick has embodied the quest for experience in a form essentially innocent. For Rowland the statue possesses "the beauty of natural movement; nothing had been sought to be represented but the perfection of an attitude" (NY, I:17–18). The similarity of this to his later description of Christina, after she has at his instigation broken with Roderick, is striking: "She's an actress, she could n't forego doing it with a flourish, and it was just the flourish that made it work wrong. I wished her of course to let him down easy; but she must have the curtain drop on an attitude, and her attitudes don't in the least do for inflammable natures" (NY, I:297).

Christina is, like Roderick, an artist in that she is the creator of "attitudes," with the difference that her medium is herself—or it might be more appropriate to say that she attempts to create herself out of attitudes. Like the statue which figures for Roderick, she has a thirst for the world's experience—attributable though it may be to an overdose of the world, rather than to a lack of it—which will be largely responsible for her undoing. Her repetition of the cup image underscores the similarity of her predicament to Roderick's: "It was on the one side the world, the splendid, beautiful, powerful, interesting world. I know what that is; I've tasted of the cup; I like its sweetness. . . . Ah, what a pity that could n't be too!" (NY, I:406–407). Christina's rich confrontation of the mutually exclusive claims of the world and the would-be self parallels and heightens the dilemma of Roderick's innocent genius faced with the experience of the world.

Roderick's first two productions after he has been in Rome are almost blatantly emblematic of his innocence—the great Adam and Eve. Thereafter his work undergoes a significant change. As Edwin T. Bowden has observed: "There is . . . a firmly established symbolism in which each of Roderick Hudson's sculptures defines one phase of the young sculptor's career. More subtly, his sculpture often suggests elements of his own character."[2] The next sculpture he produces definitely indicates the change produced in him by his experience of the world. A large female figure, it appears significantly in the chapter entitled in the 1876 text "Experience"; and the quality in it to which Rowland Mallet objects is described in that text as "softness" (*RH*, 129), in the New York Edition as "emphasized grace" (NY, I:143). It is a quality, in both cases, opposed to the simplicity, the abstraction, the angularity of Roderick's original artistic vision, and it is associated with the ambiguous roundness which in James always connotes experience.

Roderick's creation of the new sculpture follows immediately his debut in the great world, his stay at Baden-Baden, where he learned to spend money lavishly, even in gambling it away, in pursuing the pleasures the world offers: "Roderick told how much—measured simply in vulgar cash—the mistake had cost him." Rowland immediately translates "vulgar cash" into genius: "If you've got facility, respect it, nurse it, adore it, save it up in an old stocking—don't speculate on it" (NY, I:139–140). The metaphorical equation of money and imaginative genius, suggested by the association of Rowland and Roderick, and the sense of the world's cultivation as the imagination's expense are made explicit here and will be carried throughout the novel.

Immediately following Rowland's equation, Roderick breaks forth with a pregnant enunciation:

"The will, it seems to me, is an abyss of abysses and a riddle of riddles. Who can answer for his properly having one? who can say beforehand that it's going in a given case to be worth anything at all? There are all kinds of uncanny underhand currents moving to and fro between one's will and the rest of one—one's imagination in particular. People talk as if the two things were essentially distinct; on different sides of one's organism, like the heart and the liver. Mine, I know— that is my imagination and my conscience—are much nearer together. It all depends upon circumstances. I believe there's a certain group of circumstances possible for every man, in which his power to choose is destined to snap like a dry twig." (NY, I:141)

One large draught of experience has transformed Roderick from the prophet of the vast and the infinite into the creature of particular circumstances. Something of the same sense is present in Rowland's feeling about Rome:

> It was a large, vague, idle, half-profitless emotion, of which perhaps the most pertinent thing that might be said was that it brought with it a relaxed acceptance of the present, the actual, the sensuous—of existence on the terms of the moment. It was perhaps for this very reason that, in spite of the charm which Rome flings over one's mood, there ran through Rowland's meditations an undertone of melancholy natural enough in a mind which finds its horizon sensibly limited— even by a magic circle. (NY, I:171)

The passage concludes in the original with a "horizon insidiously limited to the finite" (RH, 155).

The contrast of the European present, actual, sensuous, finite with the American timeless, romantic, abstract, infinite is strikingly made. The finitude of European experience's particularity, a finitude which permeates Roderick's sense of his genius and expresses itself in cash terms—"Who shall assure me that my credit is for an unlimited sum?" (NY, I:231)—is antithetical to the essential character of Roderick's imagination, and the book provides no tenable synthesis.

Roderick's description of his plight, following his return from Baden-Baden, gives a splendid account of his imaginative dilemma: "I have n't a blamed idea. I think of subjects, but they remain mere idiotic names. They're mere words—they're not images" (NY, I:149). He has been reduced to something like Christina's nominalism, the abstractions of his romantic American imagination have been stripped of their concreteness, their image quality (and that his aesthetic images are in a sense "concrete universals" seems obvious) by his exposure to the rich welter of Roman particularity.

One possible synthesis is almost pointed up in the novel. Roderick does after all have one subsequent artistic success (leaving out of consideration the bust of his mother, which is a sheer "American" product)—the bust of Christina Light. Roderick has told Christina, "Mademoiselle, you almost satisfy my conception of the beautiful" (RH, 153), and it is as the object of the romantic imagination, as the embodiment of the beautiful, that he does her. His attitude after he has completed the bust, however, radically shifts: "I've quite forgotten her beauty, or rather I've ceased to perceive it as something distinct and defined, something independent of the rest of her. She's all one, and all impossibly interesting" (NY, I:187). She is no longer just the object of his imagination; the confusion of will and imagination which he has previously noted has become fully operative, and he now desires her. But the act of will toward Christina stifles his imagination. Roderick's collapse looks toward the death-blow Mann would give Kantian disinterest in *Death in Venice*, but it is even more prophetic of James's incessant attempts to resolve will and imagination, moral and aesthetic, particular and abstract, world and self. For the time, such a compromise solution as Gloriani's fashionable aestheticism is the only possible one. Roderick is destined to remain incomplete.

It is Roderick's incompleteness, a strain much played by Rowland in the course of the novel, which stands out at the end of the book—not only his perhaps unavoidable failure in coming to terms with the world, but also his failure in gaining a sense of others. This is rendered most explicitly in one of

Rowland's observations; "Of his never thinking of others save as they figured in his own drama this extraordinary insensibility to the injurious effects of his eloquence was a capital example. . . . He never saw himself as part of a whole; only as the clear-cut, sharp-edged, isolated individual, rejoicing or raging, as the case might be, but needing in any case absolutely to affirm himself" (NY, I:429). His sharp-edgedness is akin to the angularity of his genius, but it also indicates the inherent limitation of his genius, his failure to observe, to see himself in relation to others. Of Rowland's incompleteness we have had ample view before, but one thing he decidedly does not lack (save in the instance of Christina's affections) is the observational power. It is Roderick's ultimate sense that he himself does lack this observational power, and his sense purely in aesthetic terms, which precipitates what may be his suicide, what is in any case his final contempt for himself. Roderick's failure to see his lack in moral terms does not indicate that it is not a moral deficiency, but rather that his aesthetic limitations may be moral ones as well (just as, conversely, some of Rowland's obtuseness may be laid to an aesthetic deficiency). The final sense of the novel, then, is one of radical incompleteness, of the immense alienation of Roderick's wealth from Rowland's, and of both from the wealth of the world.

III

The protagonist of *The American* is that *rara avis* among Jamesian heroes, the American businessman; and the action is the conversion of his business sense into something at least approximating genuine imagination. Contrasted with the transitional phase of Christopher Newman's American business sense are two European attitudes, the down-and-out mercenariness of the Nioches and the tradition-centered honor of the Bellegardes, a hollow pretense which embraces murder under the cover of respectability. That the honor of the Bellegardes is not very far removed from the unscrupulous money-grubbing of Mlle

Nioche (the Bellegardes obviously regard their acceptance of Newman's suit as a kind of prostitution) is evident in the way the old Marquise takes up Newman's professions of wealth and in the interesting juxtaposition which constitutes Urbain's praise of Lord Deepmere: "But Lord Deepmere's title is English and his English property immense. He is a charming young man" (Am, 235).

In the New York Edition preface to *The American* James sees the "romance" necessities of the context for his hero's final gesture as a contradiction of what should have been a logical extension of the Bellegardes' avidity: "They would positively have jumped then, the Bellegardes, at my rich and easy American, and not have 'minded' in the least any drawback . . . taking with alacrity everything he could give them, only asking for more and more, and then adjusting their pretensions and their pride to it with all the comfort in life" (NY, II:xix–xx). But that presumptive extension, because of the author's manipulation to accommodate his *donnée*, is missing from the novel; and the existing irony is left to attend the rejection by the Bellegardes of a commerciality which falls far short of their own— the aversion of a spiritual avidity for the fact of Newman's washtubs.

The conversion of Newman's business sense has begun prior to the action of the novel. He has had, during the course of a cab ride, an extraordinary epiphany whereby he has let pass the chance of beating an adversary out of sixty thousand dollars on the stock market: "The idea of losing that sixty thousand dollars, of letting it utterly slide and scuttle and never hearing of it again, seemed the sweetest thing in the world. And all this took place quite independently of my will, and I sat watching it as if it were a play at the theatre" (Am, 32). Previously money had been for him an end in itself, its acquisition postulated by his will:

> It must be admitted, rather nakedly, that Christopher Newman's sole aim in life had been to make money; what he had been placed in the world for was, to his own perception, simply

to wrest a fortune, the bigger the better, from defiant opportunity. This idea completely filled his horizon and satisfied his
imagination. Upon the uses of money, upon what one might
do with a life into which one had succeeded in injecting the
golden stream, he had up to his thirty-fifth year very scantily
reflected. (Am, 28–29)

Miraculously, however, in the cab scene, the horizons of his
imagination have suddenly expanded and outstripped his will,
giving him a double sense of himself: the customary self, con-
structed by the habitually unquestioned postulations of the will,
viewing the transformation as an external spectacle, while the
mysteriously awakened imagination sees the proposed course of
the customary self as untenable and its postulated end as illu-
sive. This first epiphany (rather hard to buy in its simply re-
ported form) results in the renunciation of vengeance conceived
in cash terms, just as the second epiphany will result in the
renunciation of vengeance conceived in ethical terms. Newman
gains simultaneuosly an imaginative sense of himself and of his
money. Money is no longer something to be acquired as sheer
possession, but to be used in developing the possibilities of the
self. It thus becomes the symbolic equivalent of those possibilities.

Newman has come, then, an empty but capacious and
yearning receptacle, to fill himself with the multifarious stuffs
of Europe, to which new end his money will be the means: "I
know the best can't be had for mere money, but I rather think
money will do a good deal. In addition, I am willing to take a
good deal of trouble" (Am, 34). However, there is more than
a hint of the old commercialism here, and in the New York
Edition James softens it by throwing out what money will do
and coordinating Newman's trouble with the first clause: "I
know the best can't be had for mere money, but I'm willing to
take a good deal of trouble" (NY, II:33). Newman's conversion, in fact—and this is just as true in the New York Edition—
has been by no means complete. His new-found and struggling
idealism has not been able to break with the forms and termi-

nology of his previous way of life, as what at the outset of the book constitutes the entirety of his French vocabulary, "Combien?" (Am, 9), nicely indicates. His American absolutism is tainted with grossness: "I want the biggest kind of entertainment a man can get. People, places, art, nature, everything! I want to see the tallest mountains, and the bluest lakes, and the finest pictures, and the handsomest churches, and the most celebrated men, and the most beautiful women" (Am, 34).[3]

It is painfully abstract and quantitative, his desire for experience—an uncomprehending longing for the European aesthetic which finds a tonally similar converse in Christina Light's longing for the American ethical. Newman is woefully ignorant of art, a fact well documented by Bowden,[4] as well he might be, never before in his life having been exposed to it or having even thought about it. He buys Mlle Nioche's impossible reproductions as if he could assimilate art by osmosis, though the summer's gaping at four hundred seventy churches does seem to represent an unlikely triumph of that process. His latent sensibility—or perhaps merely his desire for one—moves toward those things which, by purchasing them, he erroneously attempts to place in significant relation with himself.

Newman is uncomprehendingly trying to buy Europe, to aggrandize its treasures as a realization of himself, and even Mme de Cintré is seen as an object for sale: "What else have I toiled and struggled for all these years? I have succeeded, and now what am I to do with my success? To make it perfect, as I see it, there must be a beautiful woman perched on the pile, like a statue on a monument. . . . I want to possess, in a word, the best article in the market" (Am, 48). Newman thus falls in with the other collector figures in James. Rowland Mallet has considered buying European art treasures for the museum of "an American city" (NY, I:6), and Adam Verver, the greatest and most problematic of James's American collectors, wants to transport the European heritage in its entirety into the confines of the archetypal "American City" museum. Even Valentin de Bellegarde is "an insatiable collector" (Am, 128), but he collects the relics of a tradition which contains him, which he thoroughly understands and covertly wishes to escape. Osmond is, of course, the collector at his most unambiguous and most vicious. He and Newman are the antithetical poles of the group, yet they are strangely similar. Each tries to aggrandize what he does not understand; but Isabel is for Osmond an external extension of his already finite and determined self, while Mme de Cintré is for Newman the realization of unknown but sensed possibilities within himself.

Newman's desire to "purchase" Europe is an attempt to enter into relation with it by the directness of juxtaposition—a relation characterized, and hence denied, by his incomprehension of the elements which he tries to assimilate. If Mme de Cintré is for Newman the embodiment of those abstractions which he lumps together as "the best," she is for the novel's reader the embodiment of those traditions which Newman completely fails to understand. Oscar Cargill, among others, sees the vagueness of her characterization as one of the book's major shortcomings: "Actually, Newman's values would have been increased by a clearer definition of what he valued."[5] But the truth is that there is little correlation between what Newman values and what Mme de Cintré is, so that what we get, given Newman as center of consciousness, is not an understanding of her nature but his inability to understand the sheer fact of her as presented to him. We do not know her as a character because she is forever muffled in those traditions which have produced her; we feel her largely as the converging point of those traditions' pressures. The love affair's implausibility, an undeniable characteristic of one's experience of the novel, is largely due to Newman's sheer incomprehension of her. On those few occasions when Mme de Cintré is directly presented in her own words, we can sense a woman who is drawn to the expansive Newman because he represents a liberation from that environment which has shaped her and which constrains her. The rest of the time she is either a bundle of Newman's abstractions or an emblem of her heritage—views which, with the other, make for incongruity rather than fullness.

Newman, even after the Bellegardes' breach of faith, sees

his possibilities as unlimited. "I will be any sort of a person you want," he tells them after they have again levelled the charge of commerciality (*Am*, 326). But the rest of the novel presents his discovery of his limits and his emancipation from a commerciality which, ironically, is not that which the Bellegardes have found repugnant. Newman's awakening in the scene with the Duchess is an acknowledgement of Europe's essential otherness, and his reflections before the house of the Carmelites in the Rue d'Enfer an acknowledgement of Claire's, the "pale, dead, discoloured wall" (*Am*, 467) an effective symbol of her oppressively final, inevitable enclosure by those forces which have all along rendered her unknowable to him. Between these two scenes we have witnessed the total extinction of Newman's commerciality:

> If, however, his commercial imagination was dead, he felt no contempt for the surviving actualities begotten by it. He was glad he had been prosperous and had been a great man of business rather than a small one; he was extremely glad he was rich. . . . If it was possible to think too much about buying and selling, it was a gain to have a good slice of life left in which not to think about them. (*Am*, 462)

Urbain, in the New York Edition, refers to Newman's plan of revealing the note as "hawking" (*NY*, II:501), and Newman's renunciation of it in effect identifies the commercial spirit with European otherness. On his return to America, "he not only puzzled the gentlemen on the stock exchange, but he was himself surprised at the extent of his indifference" (*Am*, 464). The discovery of his imagination's limits is the casting out of what was alien to it and the recognition, in his final gesture, of its true nature.

IV

The Europeans is a Jamesian satyr play, a light and ironic pendant to the more substantial and serious *Roderick Hudson* and *The American*. In its near-satirical treatment of James's pet themes, it is reminiscent of Mann's two Wagnerian parodies, "Tristan" and "The Blood of the Walsungs," though James's handling is more delicate and loving than Mann's. The familiar international situation is stood on its head, with Europe (or rather, as the case so often is in James, Europeanized America) descending on America to gather the spoils thereof. American innocence is virtually reduced to benevolent simplemindedness and European experience to casual hedonism and genial rapacity. Felix and Eugenia are of course akin to Valentin de Bellegarde and Christina Light,[6] but it is hard to imagine the former pair being killed in a duel and driving a lover to suicide.

In the world of *The Europeans* the potentialities of human experience have been drastically limited, and it is nearly impossible to take anyone very seriously. Consequently, the point of view with which the reader inevitably sympathizes is the one which does not take people or things very seriously, that of Eugenia and Felix; and the Americans, who take at least themselves very seriously indeed, fare not a little the worse for it. In using Eugenia and Felix as focus and framework, *The Europeans* is the only one of James's novels to accept at the outset as one of its working premises a curtailed sense of human possibility, and as such it may be called his only truly comic novel. As in Mann, both conceptual groups of characters are satirized, but it is the group to which the author's protagonists customarily belong that suffers most.

The theme of money becomes in *The Europeans* a device of parody, and the values usually associated with it in James are inverted. Eugenia is so utterly and consciously acquisitive that acquisitiveness becomes almost a virtue. The first chapter of the novel contains the following conversation about the Wentworths:

> "Are you very sure they are rich?" asked Felix lightly.
> His sister slowly turned in her place, looking at him. "Heavenly powers!" she murmured. "You have a way of bringing out things!"

> "It will certainly be much pleasanter if they are rich," Felix declared.
>
> "Do you suppose if I had not known they were rich I would ever have come?"
>
> The young man met his sister's somewhat peremptory eye with his bright, contented glance. "Yes, it certainly will be pleasanter," he repeated.
>
> "That is all I expect of them," said the Baroness. "I don't count upon their being clever or friendly—at first—or elegant or interesting. But I assure you I insist upon their being rich." (*Eur*, 10)

Two pages later we are told that "she felt that she had indeed come to a strange country, to make her fortune." Another two pages on there is mention of "the Baroness, who had come to seek her fortune," and in the same paragraph it is stated that "if she had come to seek her fortune, it seemed to her that her fortune would be easy to find" (*Eur*, 12, 14). The repetition of the exact phrase—it recurs motivically at least twice again (*Eur*, 129, 161)—is so blatant that it takes the poison of moral stigma out of it. Eugenia is so consciously on the make that her end is less money itself than the role of seeking it, one of the many roles which she plays.

The Wentworths have as much money as Eugenia has anticipated, but, like the early Newman, they do not know what can be done with it, as the following conversation between Felix and Eugenia indicates:

> " . . . it's the *ton* of the golden age."
>
> "And have they nothing golden but their *ton*? Are there no symptoms of wealth?"
>
> "I should say there was wealth without symptoms. A plain, homely way of life; nothing for show, and very little for —what shall I call it?—for the senses; but a great *aisance*, and a lot of money, out of sight, that comes forward very quietly for subscriptions to institutions, for repairing tenements, for paying doctor's bills; perhaps even for portioning daughters." (*Eur*, 35)

Eugenia, on the other hand, has symptoms without wealth, and the statement would be a ready symbolic condemnation of her were this any other of James's novels than *The Europeans*. As it is, though one can grant that "repairing tenements" is not an endeavor to be scoffed at (the phrase, however, seems here to mean restoring them to their original state of "tenement-ness"), the tone of the Europeanized brother and sister is so infectious that one cannot help feeling what the Wentworths do with their money to be, at least, pretty tame. The Wentworth household seems "to be founded upon a degree of material abundance for which, in certain matters of detail, one might have looked in vain at the frugal little court of Silberstadt-Schreckenstein" (*Eur*, 57–58), but it is Eugenia rather than the Wentworths who represents the principle of abundance in the novel.

Richard Poirier has pointed out that Eugenia "must, to be honest with herself, keep all her motives at play and never give herself coarsely to one of them."[7] To agree, however, is not to grant her any the less ironically conceived. Her tone covers her, and it covers her failure to make her fortune. "As always," says Poirier of James, "his preference is for inclusiveness,"[8] but the inclusiveness represented by Eugenia accepts as a limit the facts of experience. It includes the world's forms, but it excludes certain forms of human aspiration which are antithetical to them. Eugenia, in short, knows from the beginning what she can make of herself and how she can use the material wealth of the world to make it, and James, for once, accepts such limits as termini for imaginative inquiry. In the first of James's masterpieces, the excluded territory of *The Europeans* became the province for examination as Isabel Archer explores the commensurability of the infinitely inclusive self with a world figured as cold cash.

CHAPTER FOUR

The Portrait of a Lady

I am what is around me.

Women understand this.
One is not a duchess
a hundred yards from a carriage.

These, then are portraits:
a black vestibule;
a high bed sheltered by curtains.

These are merely instances.

— Wallace Stevens

I

"But for her money, as she saw to-day," muses Isabel Archer in her great vigil before the dying fire, "she would never have done it" (NY, IV:192). Her inheritance from Mr. Touchett, which was to have been the guarantee of that personal freedom which Isabel has from the beginning of the novel claimed for herself, has been the means, in fact, whereby she has virtually imprisoned herself:

> At bottom her money had been a burden, had been on her mind, which was filled with the desire to transfer the weight of it to some other conscience, to some more prepared receptacle. What would lighten her own conscience more effectually than to make it over to the man with the best taste in the world? . . . He would use her fortune in a way that would make her think better of it and rub off a certain grossness at-

taching to the good luck of an unexpected inheritance. There had been nothing very delicate in inheriting seventy thousand pounds; the delicacy had been all in Mr. Touchett's leaving them to her. But to marry Gilbert Osmond and bring him such a portion—in that there would be delicacy for her as well. There would be less for him—that was true; but that was his affair, and if he loved her he would not object to her being rich. (NY, IV:193)

The passage is a telling one, particularly because it is the reader's first access in well over three hundred pages to Isabel's reflections on her fortune, and the force of it rather pulls him up in seeming to contradict his sense of how Isabel sees her wealth. Her meditation reveals that her fortune has been from the moment she inherited it not the symbolic equivalent of her freedom, the means of satisfying the demands of her imagination, but an impingement on that freedom, that imagination. The delicacy has attended Mr. Touchett's giving the money, not her receiving it.

The value of money, then, appears less an intrinsic property than a function of one's relation with it. To possess it is, for Isabel, to be weighted down by it; only in giving her fortune away can she, at least for herself, free it of its material grossness and allow it to achieve a sort of symbolic equivalence with the better possibilities of herself. So Isabel sees her money, and there is something a little startling in her consciously imposing on the man she loves a burden of which she is eager to free herself. For "she had loved him," she reflects during the same vigil, " . . . a good deal for what she found in him, but a good deal also for what she brought him and what might enrich the gift" (NY, IV:192). The latter ambiguous clause means the enrichment which attends the giving, the imaginative conversion of the gift in the giving, as well as the enrichment of his own great taste which Osmond was to have brought; but the ambiguity goes beyond Isabel's own ellipsis.

Lyall H. Powers sees Isabel as having "bought" Osmond, as an acquisitor of the Osmondian order,[1] and it may be that she has been of the devil's party without knowing it. That order and that possibility, however, await further clarification. What presses here is that Isabel's sense of her money, surprising though it may be, is perfectly prepared for, perfectly consistent with her presentation in the novel to this point. The surprise lies largely in the suppression hitherto of Isabel's sense of her money and in the reader's overwhelming awareness of Ralph's sense of it as the ultimate liberation of Isabel's consciousness. That it is finally no such thing for Isabel is perfectly indicated by her immediate reaction to her inheritance:

> Isabel thought very often of the fact of her accession of means, looking at it in a dozen different lights; but we shall not now attempt to follow her train of thought or to explain exactly why her new consciousness was at first oppressive. This failure to rise to immediate joy was indeed but brief; the girl presently made up her mind that to be rich was a virtue because it was to be able to *do*, and that to do could only be sweet. . . . The acquisition of power made her serious; she scrutinised her power with a kind of tender ferocity, but was not eager to exercise it. (NY, III:300–301)

The explanation, as a matter of fact, is postponed until the stock-taking of Chapter XLII, but that Isabel should withdraw from the exercise of power which possession of the money entails, that her conception of freedom rests on the antithesis of "doing," is the burden of the novel to this point. "To be able to *do*" is one thing, is sweet, is precisely Isabel's "freedom"; to *do* is quite another, for the doing imposes a limit on the self's ability to do. Isabel's theory of her freedom leads her to a covert flirtation with the antithetical theory of Madame Merle.[2]

The exposition of these two theories concerning the nature of the self occurs immediately prior to Mr. Touchett's death and Isabel's discovery of her inheritance. Their juxtaposition at such a crucial point (at the end of what one might call the novel's exposition) is hardly accidental, and its significance is sharply pointed in a nicely ironic epilogue to the major conversation. Madame Merle, deftly analyzing Isabel, takes her to task:

"You appear to have the vaguest ideas about your earthly possessions; but from what I can make out you're not embarrassed with an income. I wish you had a little money."

"I wish I had!" said Isabel, simply, apparently forgetting for the moment that her poverty had been a venial fault for two gallant gentlemen. (NY, III:290)

A tension in Isabel, almost a contradictoriness, which is related to her theory of the self and which manifests itself frequently in her trying out the roles of others,[3] is evident here, especially in the light of the preceding conversation. That conversation's importance in the novel has been made abundantly clear by Frederick C. Crews,[4] and the passage is a familiar one; still, as it bears on virtually all of our analysis, it had better be quoted at length here:

"When you've lived as long as I you'll see that every human being has his shell and that you must take the shell into account. By the shell I mean the whole envelope of circumstances. There's no such thing as an isolated man or woman; we're each of use made up of some cluster of appurtenances. What shall we call our 'self'? Where does it begin? where does it end? It overflows into everything that belongs to us—and then it flows back again. I know a large part of myself is in the clothes I choose to wear. I've a great respect for *things*! One's self—for other people—is one's expression of one's self; and one's house, one's furniture, one's garments, the books one reads, the company one keeps—these things are all expressive."

. . . Isabel was fond of metaphysics, but was unable to accompany her friend into this bold analysis of the human personality. "I don't agree with you. I think just the other way. I don't know whether I succeed in expressing myself, but I know that nothing else expresses me. Nothing that belongs to me is any measure of me; everything's on the contrary a limit, a barrier, and a perfectly arbitrary one. Certainly the clothes which, as you say, I choose to wear, don't express me; and heaven forbid they should!"

"You dress very well," Madame Merle lightly interposed.

"Possibly; but I don't care to be judged by that. My clothes may express the dressmaker, but they don't express me. To begin with it's not my own choice that I wear them; they're imposed upon me by society."

"Should you prefer to go without them?" Madame Merle

enquired in a tone which virtually terminated the discussion.
(NY, III:287–288)

The conversation is a gloss on everything that has so far
passed in the novel and everything that is to happen—above
all, on Isabel's rejection of Lord Warburton, on her impending
acceptance of Osmond. The independent, inexpressible self of
Isabel is about to be given an envelope of circumstances in the
fortune which Mr. Touchett leaves her at Ralph's prompting,
and the remainder of the novel is an examination of what she
does with that envelope and what the consequences of that
action are—how, for her, appurtenances can only be expressive
if converted into gesture. The about-face which Isabel performs
in the immediately ensuing conversation indicates the naïveté
of a fine priorism which seemingly wavers and almost knuckles
under at the first touch of its opposite; but the line she takes in
the debate on the self is the credo which, in large measure, determines what becomes of her. Such language possibly suggests
that a belief can be as much an appurtenance as a fortune, and
raises the question whether there is anything intrinsic to the
self or whether what is called the self is simply a spatio-tem-
poral series of accumulations. Such questions will necessarily
figure importantly in our analysis.

For *The Portrait of a Lady*, if it must be said to be about
something, is surely about the problem of the self, a problem
which achieves full concretion only in the fact of Isabel's inheritance. The conversation between Madame Merle and Isabel
is only the most explicit discussion of an issue which occupies
the thought and conversation of almost all the characters
throughout the novel. Here the lines are most distinctly drawn,
here the antithetical positions most firmly codified; but the rest
of the novel's conversation and meditation seeds the ideas here
crystallized, the rest of its action develops and interrelates
them.

Isabel and Madame Merle are by no means the only characters who speculate on the subject. "I like to be treated as an

individual; you like to be treated as a 'party,' " says Mrs. Touchett to Henrietta Stackpole, who replies, "I like to be treated as an American lady." Lord Warburton, whose political views are an attempted atonement for his social position, observes "how I should object to myself if I were not myself." Ralph hypothesizes that the self is, to an extent, determined: "Ah, one does n't give up one's country any more than one gives up one's grandmother. They're both antecedent to choice —*elements of one's composition that are not to be eliminated*" (NY, III:134, 182, 125).[5] The nature of the self is at the center of the thoughts and actions of all the characters, but the movement of its centrality for Isabel from the sheerly problematic to the confrontingly actual comes only when it must meet the threat of her fortune, Madame Merle's "envelope" become nearly intractable fact. The confrontation depends, however, as does the defining conversation with Madame Merle, upon the basis of Isabel's sense of her self, and it will be necessary to see what money catalyzes before investigating how it does so.

II

The question of the self in *The Portrait of a Lady* turns essentially on the question of freedom, one which has elicited a good deal of seemingly irreconcilable comment on the part of critics. Two opinions illustrate the problem here. Yvor Winters sees James as having attempted to place his central characters, such as Isabel, in situations which permit them maximal freedom in order "to create the illusion of unhampered choice." For him, "Isabel Archer is benevolently provided with funds after her story opens, with the express purpose that her action shall thereafter be unhampered."[6] Taking a different line, Oscar Cargill resolves the novel's difficulties by seeing James as having placed Isabel within the "gallery of *limited* heroines"[7] and attributing Isabel's seeming peculiarities of behavior to the limits which the author has placed upon her. That both of these opinions are in a sense right and that it is perfectly legitimate to speak of an author's giving freedom to or imposing limitations upon a character cannot be gainsaid; but to confuse the freedom or limitation imposed by the author with these concepts as they appear in the novel is to move from one level of discourse to another, a dangerous move unless our sense of each level and of the distance between is sufficiently clear.[8]

That James was doing with Isabel something of what Winters attributes to him is obvious from the preface to *Portrait*, but that her provision of funds leaves her unhampered can be categorically denied. The funds leave her unhampered with the need to acquire funds, but they leave her hampered with themselves. Winters attributes (in part rightly) to James Ralph's view that the money is the means to Isabel's freedom; what he neglects is what the money means for Isabel, what her sense of freedom is. In short, "freedom," "money," the rest of the novel's important terms await the definition and development of the book's movement, are meaningful only in the characters' sense of them and the projection of that sense into action. What "freedom" means for Isabel is dependent upon what she conceives the nature of her self to be, and both her sense and that which Winters attributes to James are subject to the test of the novel's experience.

Similarly, Cargill's resolution of the novel's admitted problems by relegating Isabel to the category of "limited heroines," despite a thorough listing of "limitations," seems a sidestepping of one of the novel's central issues—the meaning of the concept of limit in relation to the individual human being. That Isabel is limited, or finite, is of course a truism. So are all people and all other fictional characters (even Milton's God, though infinite by definition, is presentationally finite). That she is limited in a more ordinary sense of the term—in other words, that she "has her limitations"—is more what Cargill means, but to say that is simply to classify her as a fallible human being.

That Isabel regards herself as in a sense unlimited is a point at which the modern reader consciously balks at suspending his disbelief, though the sense of an infinitude of personal possibility is probably not completely foreign to even the most devout behaviorist. Historical criticism can, I suppose, happily be invoked at this point; certainly that Isabel Archer's view of herself and the world has a good deal to do with American Transcendentalism; that the climate of ideas which surrounded her development and that of her creator is precisely one of those limits which the ideas themselves would deny,[9] are hardly questionable and critically quite useful. To solve Isabel's problems, however, by associating her with a literary or intellectual tradition will not exactly do. Rather, we must cancel as far as possible our awareness of any extrinsic notions of freedom (or its absence) and limitation and submit ourselves wholly to Isabel's, which are corrolaries of her notion of the self. In discussing a novel which is to a large degree about the evolution of limit as a concept for the central character, it is an oversimplification to postulate her initial limitation as the cause of the novel's action. This is to beg, beyond the question, the entirety of the book.

One must, in attempting to determine the significance of a concept such as freedom in the *Portrait*, heed the warning of Richard Poirier, who has stressed the dangerous tendency in the criticism of American fiction to extract patterns of imagistic or intellectual significance and to neglect the dramatic continuum of character in action[10]—the representation, as James would have it, of "felt life." Such criticism, which eschews the novel as the portrayal of "real" characters in action in favor of the novel as verbal construct, tends to turn any book into a philosophical allegory, with each character standing for some choice abstraction. Thus Kate Croy and Marian Condrip in *The Wings of the Dove* are, in Quentin Anderson's terms, "selfhood" and the "cloacal church" without quite being Kate Croy and Marian Condrip. Similarly, Isabel Archer might be the "autonomous self," Madame Merle "the socially defined self." Poirier's point is that one should not take everything Isabel, for instance, says with complete seriousness; that what she says is not necessarily true of the novel's world nor of herself; that the context of the statement and Isabel's prior history and motivations condition any remarks she may make—that, in short, a valid interpretation of the novel cannot be built on a series of quotations confronted in isolation.

We cannot assert, therefore, that Isabel's long disquisition on the nature of the self is an accurate description of what in the novel "the self" is, of what she herself is, or even of what she believes "the self" or "herself" to be. But it is undeniable that what she says has a good deal to do with what she believes (and what she believes obviously has a good deal to do with what she is) and that by examining what she says in the context of what she does we can find out a good deal about Isabel Archer and, consequently, about what she signifies—or what her words and actions signify—in the world of *The Portrait of a Lady*. We can thus to a degree avoid the equation of Isabel with any abstract concept of the self and simply see her as someone called a self, calling herself a self—with certain beliefs, sometimes in accord with her behavior, sometimes in conflict with it, regarding the nature of the self. By examining the interaction of professed belief and behavior, their reciprocal illuminations and contradictions, we may gain a firmer grasp on both character and pattern, may even see their identity and inextricability, which is finally another way of stating the novel's theme.

The central conversation between Isabel and Madame Merle provides a concentration of many of the novel's key terms, among them two which have received elaborate development up to that point: *choice* and *judgement*. Isabel's statement that "the clothes which, as you say, I choose to wear, don't express me" seems, particularly in regard to the simple word "choose," innocent enough, incapable of carrying any portentous significance, yet it gathers together the innumerable references to choosing, the innumerable instances of choice and abstention from choice, which have preceded it, and indicates something rather important about Isabel. Here Isabel assents to her freedom of choice in her clothes but denies that the clothes which she has chosen over others are any measure of her, have any significant relation to herself. The self is for her autonomous, independent even of its own choices, independent (if the theory is taken to its extreme) of the external history of Isabel Archer, a history which is composed of choices made. In this instance Isabel is defending the integrity of her spiritual self—a constant which is at the same time mysteriously capable of actualizing unlimited potential—from the impingement of material reality.

"I don't care to be judged by that," she replies to Madame Merle's charge that she dresses well, she who insists on judging everyone not for his position in the world or what surrounds him but for what he "is," the self divorced from the phenomenal envelope. Isabel thus repudiates her own good taste as a criterion for judgement—the same Isabel who will see herself as having made her fortune over "to the man with the best taste in the world." She then, however, immediately reverses herself on the question of choice: "it's not my own choice that I wear them; they're imposed upon me by society." She has backed down, realizing that to admit choice in the realm of phenomena is to admit that the phenomena chosen are to some degree indicative of one's nature. Madame Merle counters and wins the debate with "Should you prefer to go without them?" If the choice of any clothes is not expressive of Isabel's self, then would the only possible alternative, the *reductio* of going nude, be any more so? Madame Merle's parry not only takes us back to Isabel's premise that "nothing else expresses me" but also provides an answer to her "I don't know whether I succeed in expressing myself," for if no possible choice within the context of actuality is relevant to the nature of the self, then the self is inexpressible, unknowable, unjudgeable—an inner life existing within the context of, but totally unrelated to, an external reality which passes for the manifestation of it. Such absolutism necessarily turns out to be solipsism, and from that viewpoint it is small wonder Henrietta gets so slight a view of the "inner life." Something like this finally seems to be the meaning of that freedom of Isabel's upon which her fortune will impinge, but its full sense is revealed only through the series of judgements and choices which bring her out at such a point.

A tendency to reverse her professed position, as in the above passage, is characteristic of Isabel and makes an assessment of what she actually believes somewhat difficult, but the contradiction of statement points to the fundamental paradox at the root of her idealistic theory of the self, one which accounts for what are in fact her abstentions from choice and judgement in the novel's expository portion.

Among the first things we hear from Isabel upon her arrival at Gardencourt is her somewhat baffled response at being confronted with the relative merits of Gardencourt and Lockleigh: "I don't know—I can't judge" (NY, III:22). The naïve girl fresh from America is at a loss to discriminate between the various phenomenal forms which Europe immediately presents her (she has, of course, not yet even seen Lockleigh), and her comment may be no more than a profession of inexperience or an attempt to avoid being impolite to either Mr. Touchett or Lord Warburton. What seems merely a social gesture is, however, underlined as something more by Isabel's first sedentary excursion into her past, the precursor of the vigil in Chapter XLII, in the flashback of Chapter IV, after Mrs. Touchett has announced her intention of taking Isabel to Europe:

> The importance of what had happened was out of proportion to its appearance; there had really been a change in her life. What it would bring with it was as yet extremely indefinite; but Isabel was in a situation that gave a value to any change. She had a desire to leave the past behind her and, as she said to herself, to begin afresh. This desire indeed was not a birth of the present occasion; it was as familiar as the sound of the rain upon the window and it had led to her beginning afresh a great many times. She closed her eyes as she sat in one of the dusky corners of the quiet parlour; but it was not with a desire for dozing forgetfulness. It was on the contrary because she . . . wished to check the sense of seeing too many things at once. Her imagination was by habit ridiculously active; when the door was not open it jumped out the window.

She was not accustomed indeed to keep it behind bolts; and at important moments, when she would have been thankful to make use of her judgment alone, she paid the penalty of having given undue encouragement to the faculty of seeing without judging. (NY, III:41–42)

Several things stand out here. The first, the disparity between apparent and real, external and internal significance, looks ahead to the breakdown between the "inner life" and the life lived in the world and lays the ground for the mental predicament which immediately follows. Isabel desires a change, desires to renounce the nearly blank page of her past and to "begin afresh," to embark on a new history which will be more commensurate with the demands of her real nature.[11] This desire indicates that Isabel believes (the "metaphysical" discussion bears out the belief) her past to be completely irrelevant to her self—even though, two pages later, the reader will be treated to her perversely defensive "sense" that "her opportunities had been large" (NY, III:43)—a set of conditions imposed upon the realization of her potentialities but in no way determinant of what those potentialities are. The change she wishes is external; she herself cannot change, but she can move into a context of circumstances which will allow her to manifest more fully the attributes inherent in her all the time. If such a wish directly contradicts her later expression of what we might call the principle of nonexternalization, the contradiction is implied, we shall see, in the very nature of her theory of the self.

Such in any case is Isabel's overriding sense of herself, a sense identified with her imagination, the faculty "of seeing too many things at once," of entertaining simultaneously possibilities which are perhaps mutually exclusive. Isabel notes the danger of her imagination, or the narrator notes it for her (it is "ridiculously active"), and she realizes that she is prone to "seeing without judging." "Seeing" here appears to mean the imaginative approach, the mental stance of the observer capable of maintaining all possibles, even contradictory ones, without

excluding any. Judgement, on the other hand, as Isabel conceives it, is a choice between possibles and the rejection of
some. It is the actualization of one of the imagination's potentialities, but in the fact of its selectivity it is necessarily exclusive and hence a misrepresentation of the self, a limitation
which the self imposes upon itself.

Isabel is, of course, not yet aware of her philosophical
quandary. She will, in fact, very shortly after ride roughshod
over it in her famous demand of Mrs. Touchett that she be
told what things are improper "so as to choose" whether to do
them or not (NY, III:93). The freedom to choose, to judge,
is a necessary aspect of Isabel's idea of herself as an independent entity. The question she evades here in the heat of her self-
assertion is the one at the bottom of her Albany meditation,
the question of what happens to freedom in the act of choice,
of judgement. It is one which her unchosen acquisition of
funds, the agency necessitating action in a world of choice, will
make her face, though her effort to do so will amount primarily
to an attempt at translating the question into her own language.

Isabel's present desire, however, as James gives it to us in
the lovingly critical appraisal of her character which begins
Chapter VI—one which naïvely skirts the paradoxes of its entailments—is that "she would be what she appeared, and she
would appear what she was," a "desire to look very well and to
be if possible even better" (NY, III:69). This flight is typical
of the early Isabel in her aspiring, noncritical mood—a mood
which brushes aside the particularities of choice for the vague-
nesses of romantic projection, which postulates a fusion of appearance and reality, the perfect externalization of a perfect if
nascent self. "She had a fixed determination," we are told, "to
regard the world as a place of brightness, of free expansion, of
irresistible action" (NY, III:68). In short, Isabel sees the world
as the context for, rather than the limit upon, her freedom, a
freedom to be manifested (though "fixed determination" ironically undercuts the idea) in the inclusive and irresistible action
of expansion. The world is simply read as the surrogate of, the

correspondent to the self; and that self, to Isabel's elated understanding of it, is little more than possibility expressible in action—though action in the abstract, as she will come to realize,
receives its denial in particular actions.

Action is, however, in this portion of the novel, totally sus-
pended, for any action of hers would become, as an expression
of choice and judgement made, a limitation imposed upon what
Isabel thinks herself to be, an apparent *definiens* belying the
amplitude of the *definiendum*. Isabel can, therefore—must,
therefore, one is tempted to say—project herself imaginatively
into the world of action, flirting with alternative modes of externalization—"I suppose I'm rather versatile. I like people to
be totally different from Henrietta—in the style of Lord Warburton's sisters for instance. So long as I look at the Misses
Molyneux they seem to me to answer a kind of ideal. Then
Henrietta presents herself and I'm straightway convinced by
her" (NY, III:130), or "I 'm a little on the side of everything"
(NY, III:100)—and refrain at the same time from committing
herself to choice or judgement, any choice or judgement, that
is, which would in effect commit her. As David Marcell says in
his fine essay on the *Portrait*, "*The desire to be limitless becomes in itself a limitation*."[12]

Such a paradoxical suspension is the condition for the early
portion of the novel, in which the sense of Isabel's potentiality
is balanced by a sense of her holding in check the actualization
of her potential, in which judgements, discriminations, choices
to be made abound but are undercut by the choice which is the
relief from the necessity of choosing—the maintenance of freedom in the suspension of its operation.

For Ralph, whose awareness of the limitations which conditions have imposed upon his own freedom is strong, Isabel
is largely the aspiring spirit of expansive possibility (unlike
other women, who more or less passively await their destiny,
she will "do something" with herself), and it is this sense
which will prompt his urging his father to leave her a fortune.
For the reader, however, that passivity which Ralph finds lack-

ing in Isabel is abundantly there as the dark obverse of her
imagination's projected activity.[13] It is hinted in the conclusion
of one of Isabel's early conversations with Mr. Touchett, a conversation centering upon the fixity of form in English life and
looking forward to the issues involved in Warburton's proposal:

> "They've got everything pretty well fixed," Mr. Touchett
> admitted. "It's all settled beforehand—they don't leave it to
> the last moment."
>
> "I don't like to have everything settled beforehand," said
> the girl. "I like more unexpectedness." (NY, III:78)

The exchange is in part simply occasion for Isabel's display of
her mettle and her assertion of the American sense of possibility and adventure drastically impeded and even stultified by
British preconception. It is also an expression of what seems
less the desire to manifest individuality in action than the unconscious wish to be submitted to those conditions, unforeseen
by oneself, which will in large measure relieve one of the necessity of choosing what course of action to take.

The most notable expression of passivity on Isabel's part
occurs in an exchange (mentioned by a good many critics but
not treated very satisfactorily by any of them[14]) with Henrietta
subsequent to the interview with Goodwood in London. Henrietta is urging upon Isabel the foolishness of her having refused
Goodwood:

> "Do you know where you're going, Isabel Archer?"
>
> "Just now I'm going to bed," said Isabel with persistent
> frivolity.
>
> "Do you know where you're drifting?" Henrietta pur-
> sued. . . .
>
> "No, I have n't the least idea, and I find it very pleasant
> not to know. A swift carriage, of a dark night, rattling with
> four horses over roads that one can't see—that's my idea of
> happiness." (NY, III:235)

The strain of the encounter with Goodwood, her irritated sense
of Henrietta's having betrayed her, her "persistent frivolity," a
perverse desire to say at the moment nothing consequential or
even relevant—all these to a degree motivate what Isabel says

and qualify the significance which one assign to it. Nevertheless, if there is a perversity in what Isabel claims to be her idea of happiness, it is a perversity inherent in the quality of her imagination, which does indeed aspire to the swiftness of motion. That motion, however, is less the self's active projection into the world than its submission to unknown conditions, its allowing itself to be determined by the external—attempting to maintain its potential freedom by abstaining from that freedom's exercise only, in the maintenance, to render it subject to those conditions which actively deny it.

Even if Isabel's intent, then, is primarily frivolous, her expression is perfectly in accord with her retreat from the threat presented by Goodwood and with the sources of her desire for a maintained independence. The frivolity, if it is frivolity, is a projection, not necessarily conscious, of an essential component of her sense of selfhood—a passivity which is the mirror image of her proposed activity. As William H. Gass puts it: "There is in Isabel herself a certain willingness to be employed, a desire to be taken up and fancied, if only because that very enslavement, on other terms, makes her more free."[15]

Such is the unknown which Isabel wills in willing her own freedom, an unknown portentously hinted as she makes her first visit to Osmond's Florentine villa: "Isabel waited, with a certain unuttered contentedness, to have her movements directed; she liked Mr. Osmond's talk, his company: she had what always gave her a very private thrill, the consciousness of a new relation" (NY, III:374). The contentedness with which she waits to have her movements directed hearkens back to her "idea of happiness" and hints part of her motivation in ultimately choosing Osmond, a choice determined, in conferring the burden of her money upon him, to leave her freedom intact.

III

The question of choice in *The Portrait of a Lady* is at first the question of whom Isabel will choose for a husband, and it is the interaction of her sense of her freedom with her rejection of Lord Warburton and Caspar Goodwood which we must now examine. That Isabel should resist the obvious attractions and attributes which Warburton possesses comes as a shock primarily to Mrs. Touchett, whose notion of independence is little more than the conversion of opportunity to personal advantage. For Ralph and, to a degree, for Mr. Touchett, Isabel's rejection of Warburton is less a surprise than the confirmation of a bold originality and defiance of the conventional, a determination not to do what nine out of ten women in such a situation would do, at least not to do it for that reason. For the reader, however, who is given the privilege denied Ralph of observing Isabel's mind at work, the issues at stake present themselves as considerably more complex and inevitably involved with the paradoxes of her sense of freedom.

One might go along with Edwin T. Bowden, who sees that Isabel's "desire for complete freedom is itself a form of isolation," or with William Bysshe Stein, whose extremely unflattering portrait of James's lady depicts her as "obsessed with the abstractions of independence and freedom" to the degree that she has created for herself a "sterile femininity" all too easily the prey of Osmond's conventionality.[16] Or one can (following the line of argument previously sketched) view Isabel's decision against Warburton and her previous refraining from giving Goodwood any answer whatsoever as her choosing not to choose, preserving freedom inviolate by refraining from its exercise—the interpretation which her reference to "giving up other chances" (NY, III:186), that is, excluding other possibilities, basically indicates. Still, it is necessary to inspect Isabel's sense of the men whom she rejects so that the particular impingements upon her freedom which they represent for her may be clear.

That sense is basically an awareness of those advantages which for nine out of ten women would make Warburton an ideal husband, but for Isabel the "advantages" loom as potential threats to her cherished freedom:

She herself was a character—she could n't help being aware of that; and hitherto her visions of a completed consciousness had concerned themselves largely with moral images—things as to which the question would be whether they pleased her sublime soul. Lord Warburton loomed up before her, largely and brightly, as a collection of attributes and powers which were not to be measured by this simple rule, but which demanded a different sort of appreciation—an appreciation that the girl, with her habit of judging quickly and freely, felt she lacked patience to bestow. . . . What she felt was that a territorial, a political, a social magnate had conceived the design of drawing her into the system in which he rather invidiously lived and moved. A certain instinct, not imperious, but persuasive, told her to resist—murmured to her that virtually she had a system and an orbit of her own. (NY, III:143–144)

The antithesis evident to Isabel here is essentially the same one on which the "metaphysical" discussion with Madame Merle will turn, that of the autonomous self and the "envelope of circumstances." Christof Wegelin approaches this view when he states that "Lord Warburton's misfortune is that his eminence lies in a 'collection of attributes and powers' independent of his individual character, no matter how appealing *that* may be,"[17] though the independence of character and attribute in Warburton is Wegelin's notion rather than Isabel's.

Warburton appears to Isabel's perception not so much a self as a function of the system wherein he moves, his apparent being not an integral vessel of potentiality but a "collection of attributes" vested upon him by his position, of "powers" not inherently his. It is his fixity and finitude, evident in her regarding him as a "collection of attributes," that prompt Isabel's turning from him, a fixity and finitude inimical to the abstract flights of what James, with comprehensive irony, terms her "sublime soul." Warburton demands of her, in his proposal, an appreciation—differing in kind from her noncommitting free judgements—of an external system which not only, to her mind, defines him but also would, in the fact of her acceptance, define her. She almost instinctively reacts against being sealed up in that "envelope of circumstances" which, in effect, Warburton's offer signifies for her, observing that "in the whole there was something stiff and stupid which would make it a burden" (NY, III:144). It is the "burden" of appurtenance and limiting context which Isabel rejects in refusing Warburton, and the word will reverberate much later when she reflects upon the burden which Mr. Touchett's legacy has in fact been for her.

At this point, then, Isabel is already the unwitting advocate of Madame Merle's theory of externals, in that, for her, Warburton's involvement in what she terms his "system" is necessarily preclusive of his having a self. For Isabel's absolutism, of the logical implications of which she is at best only dimly aware, it is an all or nothing affair: any involvement with the particularity of externals becomes the extinction of the self, in that it is the self's definition. Yet the theory of externals is in fact a theory of internal relation, and as such it is necessarily entailed by Isabel's very Idealism. At this point it is for her only the vaguely realized obverse, but the movement of the novel will be toward theoretical reconciliation, toward her recognition of a viable sense of self and its relations.

If, at this point, Isabel's appreciation falls short of embracing that which masses before her as only an aggregation of fixing attributes, the appreciation of others extends at least to an awareness of the paradoxes in Warburton's own position, an awareness which assumes that the self is to a degree independent of its circumstances. Ralph, in a discussion with Isabel following her rejection of Warburton, draws a line between self and circumstances in considering the paradoxes of the British lord's situation, his liberal protestations which in effect contradict his very way of life:

> "I hope that what I said then had no weight with you; for they were not faults, the things I spoke of: they were simply peculiarities of his position. . . . I think I said that as regards that position he was rather a sceptic. It would have been in your power to make him a believer."
>
> "I think not. I don't understand the matter, and I'm not conscious of any mission of that sort." (NY, III:211)

Ralph, who has just told Isabel that Warburton "unites the intrinsic and the extrinsic advantages" (NY, III:210), differentiates between properties of the self ("faults") and properties of one's circumstances ("peculiarities of his position"). In Isabel he sees the potential of harmonizing self and circumstance, of bringing Warburton to an acceptance of his external situation and thus achieving a true union of intrinsic and extrinsic advantages—a view which looks forward to his expectations of the bequest.

Isabel, however, retreats before the question of externals into a profession of ignorance and a denial of the advocacy of a system which she has found in large measure to be a violation of her own, even though in her vaguer moments of imaginative flight she postulates a continuity of self and externality very like what Ralph has suggested she would be able to do for Warburton. Ralph's light tone is indeed an indication that Warburton's radical views are not to be taken too seriously, and his idea that Isabel could make Warburton a "believer" substantiates Isabel's own sense that Warburton is essentially the creature of the conditions within which he moves. The whole emphasis upon the paradox of Warburton's position—despite the equal emphasis upon his "intrinsic advantages," his genial and expansive nature—seems to back up the theory of external determination; and Warburton's radical views come to appear a desire for selfhood, not unlike Isabel's, antithetically generated by the conditions which they undercut.

Mr. Touchett, in an early discussion with Isabel on the subject of Warburton's "radicalism," underscores this point: "He seems to want to do away with a good many things, but he wants to remain himself. I suppose that's natural, but it's rather inconsistent." To which, with charming disregard for its implications, Isabel recites her credo: "Oh, I hope he'll remain himself" (NY, III:99). The point made by Mr. Touchett will be scored again later by Madame Merle, this time upon Isabel, in her splendidly terminal "Should you prefer to go without them?" In effect, Isabel and Warburton are in the same ideological boat, a fact which heightens both the incongruity and the necessity of Isabel's refusing him.

That refusal couches itself in a variety of terms. As Warburton presses the advantages which he can provide for Isabel and attempts to ascertain her demands, she replies, "It's not what I ask; it's what I can give" (NY, III:151·), her words looking forward to her later consideration of the delicacy attending the money she brought Osmond—the strong underlying sense in both cases being that of a burden (of externals to be "done with") transferred to other shoulders, rather than received. It is something of the same attitude which later prompts her flustered response to Mrs. Touchett's expected objections: "Do you think Lord Warburton could make me any better than I am? . . . I don't mean I'm not too good to improve. I mean—I mean that I don't love Lord Warburton enough to marry him" (NY, III:194–195). Isabel here, with seeming contrariness, sees marriage as something brought to her, an improvement in her self, rather than as an act of giving on her part, but, in her terms, the given must of necessity be the opportunity for that free expansion which she sees what Warburton would bring as effectively stifling.

The opportunity which Warburton offers is completely different, and her sense of it takes the following form:

> But though she was lost in admiration of her opportunity she managed to move back into the deepest shade of it, even as some wild, caught creature in a vast cage. The "spendid" security so offered her was *not* the greatest she could conceive. What she finally bethought herself of saying was something . . . that deferred the need of really facing her crisis (NY, III:152–153)

The passage is rather ambiguous, particularly in regard to the referent of *it*. If we take *opportunity* as antecedent (which it most probably is), then the opportunity which Warburton provides her becomes for Isabel, despite its vastness, not so much an opportunity as an imprisonment, a "cage" which prohibits her free expansion. If *admiration* is the antecedent, Isabel is paradoxically caged by her own sense of wonder at the possibilities which present themselves.

What is primarily important, however—apart from the limitation upon her freedom which Warburton's offer, in any reading, presents—is Isabel's retreating into the deepest shade of the cage, the shade redolent of that darkness into which her figurative carriage will later plunge. Though Isabel senses herself as already "caught," she rejects this potential restriction of her freedom in favor of some greater security, perhaps equally unsought but confused in her mind with the opportunity for expansion. It is finally the attempt to put off decision, or at least expression of her decision—one which, when it comes, will be the choice of abstention from choice, or at least from having chosen the finitude which Warburton to her mind represents, a decision which is ultimately but an externalization of her present indecision—that marks the moment of Isabel's dilemma, and that will issue in the "feeling of freedom" (NY, III:200), mixed as it is with her sense of having handled the matter gracelessly, dominating her consciousness in London after she has provisionally faced her crisis.

Isabel's rejection of Caspar Goodwood is a different matter from her rejection of Lord Warburton. It is, in fact less an out-and-out rejection than a continual suspension of decision, a putting off of the necessity for acceptance or rejection which typifies Isabel's preservation of her freedom in abstention from choice. Her departure for Europe with her aunt, she admits to herself in Chapter XIII (the first occasion on which the reader is given a full view of her impression of Goodwood), has been motivated by a desire not only to avail herself of the opportunity for free expansion but also to avoid having to give Goodwood a definite answer:

> Sometimes Caspar Goodwood had seemed to range himself on the side of her destiny, to be the stubbornest fact she knew; she said to herself at such moments that she might evade him for a time, but that she must make terms with him at last—terms which would be certain to be favourable to him-

self. Her impulse had been to avail herself of the things that helped her to resist such an obligation; and this impulse had been much concerned in her eager acceptance of her aunt's invitation, which had come to her at an hour when she expected from day to day to see Mr. Goodwood and when she was glad to have an answer ready for something she was sure he would say to her. (NY, III:162–163)

That the threat which Goodwood represents for Isabel is very different from Warburton's, that his impingement on her would not be in the bestowal of appurtenances, is a point recurrently emphasized. Isabel makes the contrast first as she considers the burden which Warburton's system offers:

Furthermore there was a young man lately come from America who had no system at all, but who had a character of which it was useless for her to try to persuade herself that the impression on her mind had been light. (NY, III:144)

And later, when her mind has turned more explicitly to Goodwood:

The difficulty was that more than any man she had ever known, more than poor Lord Warburton . . . , Caspar Goodwood expressed for her an energy—and she had already felt it as a power—that was of his very nature. It was in no degree a matter of his "advantages"—it was a matter of the spirit that sat in his clear-burning eyes like some tireless watcher at a window. (NY, III:162)

Goodwood is in fact an American businessman, but it is not his business imagination which Isabel fears, for she is aware of the separation between his occupation and his real nature: "He was not after all in harmony with mere smug peace and greed and gain, an order of things of which the vital breath was ubiquitous advertisement" (NY, III:164). No more than she is he externalized by his situation, though this lack of harmony—reminiscent, if only negatively, of what Ralph sees as Warburton's potential union of intrinsic and extrinsic advantage—is vaguely disquieting to her:

It struck those who knew him well that he might do greater things than carry on a cotton-factory; there was nothing cottony about Caspar Goodwood, and his friends took for granted that he would somehow and somewhere write himself in bigger letters. But it was as if something large and confused, something dark and ugly would have to call upon him. (NY, III:164)

This antithesis between Goodwood and his realm of operation is heightened upon his arrival in Rome, when Isabel has been, to a large degree, conditioned by the ideas of Osmond and Madame Merle:

Oh, he was intrinsic enough; she never thought of his even looking for artificial aids. If he extended his business—that, to the best of her belief, was the only form exertion could take with him—it would be because it was an enterprising thing, or good for the business; not in the least because he might hope it would overlay the past. This gave his figure a kind of bareness and bleakness which made the accident of meeting it in memory or in apprehension a peculiar concussion; it was deficient in the social drapery commonly muffling, in an overcivilized age, the sharpness of human contacts. (NY, IV:280)

The sharpness of human contacts has become for Isabel nothing but a source of pain—her life with her husband has done that for her—and it is the sharpness of Goodwood's selfhood which predominates in her consciousness of him. Yet that sharpness is perhaps indicative of what has motivated her retreat from him throughout the book. In her Albany phase, "her deepest enjoyment was to feel the continuity between the movements of her own soul and the agitations of the world" (NY, III:45); but the striking thing about Goodwood for her was the discontinuity between his soul and the world wherein he acted, the alienation of his self from the world of business which was his context. It was possibly the American necessity for such discontinuity which in part drove Isabel to Europe, the locus, for her, of potential expansion and externalization;

and if the extrinsic there becomes to her awareness the definer (as in the case of Warburton) or concealer ("muffling social drapery") of self, rather than its extension—if her withdrawal from Goodwood in Europe is couched in radically differing terms from those she has used in America—it is still the felt pressure of his selfhood which prompts the withdrawal.

Dorothea Krook rightly sees Isabel's rejection of Goodwood in terms both of his hardness, aggressiveness, and will to domination and of his lacking that polish and charm characteristic of such European men she meets as Lord Warburton,[18] even though these social virtues will, in their total context, prove equal drawbacks for Isabel. But it is not just Goodwood's lack of charm which makes Isabel draw back from him; it is the implication which his innate aggressiveness and his will—obvious in, though distinct from, his business activities—hold for her:

> She might like it or not, but he insisted, ever, with his whole weight and force: even in one's usual contact with him one had to reckon with that. The idea of a diminished liberty was particularly disagreeable to her at present, since she had just given a sort of personal accent to her independence by looking so straight at Lord Warburton's big bribe and yet turning away from it. (NY, III:162)

The temptation which Warburton presents is put by Isabel into financial terms, as if she were being bought or paid off with the extrinsic advantages which she sees as potentially fixing her; but the temptation and threat presented by Goodwood are more subtle and more dangerous to her mind. "Oh, he was intrinsic enough," she will admit later on, and it is his intrinsicalness, not his extrinsic positioning, which she fears. Goodwood's selfhood and will are directed to and fundamentally bound up with not the context of his business activity but Isabel herself; and it is of becoming the province of his will—her self the annexation of his—that she is afraid.

To become in a sense the externalization of Caspar Goodwood's selfhood and to submit herself to the limitations imposed by his—these are the eventualities she foresees when she considers that "however she might have resisted conquest at her English suitor's large quiet hands she was at least as far removed from the disposition to let the young man from Boston take positive possession of her" and when she rebuffs his pleas with "You've no right to talk of losing what's not yours" (NY, III: 161, 219). In short, she resists in Goodwood the same kind of aggrandizement of which she will be made unwitting prey when she makes over her fortune to the man with the best taste in the world. Such is the destiny which Goodwood appears for Isabel to align himself with, and it is her desire to avoid such a destiny that prompts her to answer him with, "I wish to choose my fate and know something of human affairs beyond what other people think it compatible with propriety to tell me" (NY, III:299), an avoidance which will eventually pitch her into the ultimate limitation of mere expressed propriety.

Isabel, in this assertion of her independence, is thrown back upon the language of choice, just as, a moment before, she has been thrown back upon that of judgement: "Besides, I try to judge things for myself; to judge wrong, I think, is more honourable than not to judge at all" (NY, III:228), and the irony lies not only in that she later will judge wrong and obtain a certain honor in the process but also in that she uses such language to avoid the very activities which it signifies. Isabel's precarious freedom now lies in her having chosen against the limitations, extrinsic and intrinsic, threatened by Warburton and Goodwood. What remains—and it is the basic action of the novel—is what she will choose for and how the basic entailments of her concept of the self will work themselves out in that choice.

IV

The choice finally made is that of Gilbert Osmond, and the agencies of that choice are the inheritance which Ralph persuades his father to leave Isabel and the influence of Madame Merle. Ralph's motives for providing Isabel a fortune have already been suggested: the money will ensure her freedom and allow her to fulfill her idea of herself, permit her the free expansion which she has sought in Europe. "If she has an easy income," Ralph argues to Mr. Touchett, "she'll never have to marry for a support. That's what I want cannily to prevent. She wishes to be free, and your bequest will make her free" (NY, III:261).

Ralph's sense of Isabel's freedom is much the same as that which Yvor Winters attributes to James; and Ralph's bestowing the fortune on Isabel is the technique whereby, as Winters would insist, the author bestows maximum freedom of choice upon his heroine. Although, as we have seen, Winters' interpretation does not consider all the complexities of the meaning of freedom in the novel, Ralph's motive is certainly, at least in part, to relieve Isabel from the necessity of submitting to material pressures, of violating her conception of herself merely in order to maintain her existence. "I call people rich when they're able to meet the requirements of their imagination," he says. "Isabel has a great deal of imagination" (NY, III:261). The fortune is to be for Ralph the material surrogate of Isabel's potentiality and the means whereby she will actualize that potentiality; the richness, to his mind, less a property bestowed in the material possession than one inherent in the self which finds externalization in the material.

In the gift Ralph is attempting for Isabel the kind of union of intrinsic and extrinsic advantages which he has sketched in the lesser case of Warburton, and he is echoing Isabel's own early wish for a felt continuity between herself and the world. What he is neglecting is the limiting relation of external fact to internal possibility which weighs so heavily on Isabel's own muddled consciousness, and his neglect is in effect the precursor of what Isabel will later sense herself to have done in bringing the fortune to Osmond. The delicacy of the conversion of brute cash into gesture is Ralph's rather than, as Isabel thinks, Mr. Touchett's, but the encumberment is in any case Isabel's. Ralph's sense of his own fortune is, of course, very different from what Isabel's sense of hers will be—money represents for him no curtailment of freedom, since his freedom is already too adequately curtailed by his ill health. The gift is in effect the bestowal upon Isabel of the very freedom he lacks, the projection upon her of his own unrealizable potential, as his final word to his father upon the subject indicates: "I shall get just the good I said a few moments ago I wished to put into Isabel's reach—that of having met the requirements of my imagination" (NY, III:265).

Several critics have been led by Ralph's attitude toward Isabel to consider him a violator of the Kantian categorical imperative of nearly Osmondian magnitude. For R. P. Blackmur, "Everybody tampers with Isabel, and it is hard to say whether her cousin Ralph Touchett, who had arranged the bequest, or the Prince [sic], Gilbert Osmond, who marries her because of it, tampers more deeply." One conclusion that can be drawn is that Isabel is equally guilty of tampering when she bestows her money on Osmond, a conclusion, as we have seen, reached by Lyall H. Powers; and indeed, as Blackmur says, "the whole novel shows how people tamper with one another because of motives that pass like money between them."[19] For William H. Gass, Ralph is an artist-type, like Osmond (though differing from him, obviously, in many respects), who occasions Isabel's imprisonment by regarding her as a means rather than as an end.[20] Ernest Sandeen, who is primarily interested in stressing the correspondence between Ralph's attitude toward Isabel and James's own attitude toward Minny Temple, stops short with seeing Ralph as an artist figure contriving Isabel's destiny.[21]

To heap upon Ralph Touchett a major share of the guilt for the fate to which Isabel succumbs is, however, considering the sympathy with which James treats him and the necessity of guilt which the net of human relations implies in The Portrait of a Lady, to distort his function in the novel, but to see where he goes awry in his appraisal of Isabel and of what he is doing for her is necessary for an understanding of that function.

We have earlier considered the disparity between Ralph's sense of his bequest for Isabel and Isabel's own sense of it—a disparity which is foreshadowed throughout the early portion of the novel by what amounts on Ralph's part to a total mis-comprehension of Isabel, fostered to some degree by Isabel's own ideal projection of herself. We have noted Isabel's with-drawal from what Ralph suggests to be her mission in regard to Warburton; and it seems clear that Ralph's attribution to Isabel of a sophisticated taste (NY, III:61) is founded less on any concrete evidence than on his desire to think that her taste seconds his own. But possibly Ralph's ultimate error in reading Isabel, a misreading upon which he founds the bequest, occurs during his long analytical exchange with her in London—a con-versation which, significantly, precedes immediately her dis-missal of Caspar Goodwood:

> "You've told me the great thing: that the world interests you and that you want to throw yourself into it."
> Her silvery eyes shone a moment in the dusk. "I never said that."
> "I think you meant it. Don't repudiate it. It's so fine!"
> "I don't know what you're trying to fasten upon me, for I'm not in the least an adventurous spirit. Women are not like men."
> . . . . "No, he said; "women rarely boast of their courage. Men do so with a certain frequency."
> "Men have it to boast of!"
> "Women have it too. You've a great deal."
> "Enough to go home in a cab to Pratt's Hotel, but not more." (NY, III:214)

That Ralph's vision of Isabel, a vision heightened by her re-fusal of Warburton, tallies with her own aspirations only heightens the irony of what he leaves out of the picture, the withdrawal into inaction which is the implied antithesis of her projected flight. Isabel's bold free spirit does indeed exist as a felt potential, but it is also in large part Ralph's creation—something which, as she charges, he is trying to fasten upon her, just as he will fasten upon her its material surrogate and agency.[22]

Ralph's is a spirit similar to Isabel's: his aspirations, his sense of freedom and expansion are very like hers; and his desire for the unexpected—"I'm extremely fond of the unexpected," he tells her (NY, III:212)—echoes that part of Isabel's romanticism which is aligned with passivity. We might, in fact, read in his illness the physical emblem of Isabel's mode of withdrawal, the condition, even the limitation, which preserves his freedom by rendering him unable to use it. But by seeing Isabel as an extension of himself (the aggrandizement which Isabel essentially fears in Goodwood) and by giving her the means to gratify her own and his imagination, he foists upon her the burden of having to define herself in terms of external action, the burden from which his physical condition relieves him and of which he is largely insensible in her. In such a manner Ralph is free not to respond to Isabel's voiced negation of what he proposes to her, to retain his image of her "fineness" and to reject her profession of cowardice, the terms of which (courage enough to go home in a cab) point ahead to the idea of happiness (the carriage) which she will articulate in the next chapter but one. In a like manner Isabel Archer will overlook Gilbert Osmond's avowals of conventionality and will in effect marry the projected concretion of her own ideals, though the extent of her misconception, even if both are made in the spirit of generosity, will be far vaster than her cousin's.

VI

The influence of Madame Merle upon Isabel, aside from the mere mechanics of her marrying Isabel to Osmond, is a profound one. Though Isabel resists the metaphysics of her older friend, she finds much in her for admiration and even emulation:

> . . . she wandered, as by the wrong side of the wall of a private garden, round the enclosed talents, accomplishments, aptitudes of Madame Merle. She found herself desiring to emulate them, and in twenty such ways this lady presented herself as a model. "I should like awfully to be so!" Isabel secretly exclaimed, more than once, as one after another of her friend's

fine aspects caught the light. . . . It took no great time indeed
for her to feel herself, as the phrase is, under an influence.
"What's the harm," she wondered, "so long as it's a good
one? The more one's under a good influence the better. The
only thing is to see our steps as we take them—to understand
them as we go. That, no doubt, I shall always do. I needn't
be afraid of becoming too pliable; isn't it my fault that I'm
not pliable enough?" It is said that imitation is the sincerest
flattery; and if Isabel was sometimes moved to gape at her
friend aspiringly and despairingly it was not so much because
she desired herself to shine as because she wished to hold up
the lamp for Madame Merle. She liked her extremely, but was
even more dazzled than attracted. (NY, III:270–271)

The passage abounds in semicontradictions and paradoxes, but
it is not surprising that Isabel's sense of herself at this point
should be somewhat contradictory. We notice her awareness
of the fact that her desire to emulate Madame Merle is inimical to her own professed independence, a fact which she tries
to circumvent by assuring herself that, submitting herself to
an outside influence as she may be, she is still in control of her
own movements ("The only thing is to see our steps as we
take them—to understand them as we go.") and which the
narrative voice qualifies in the passage on imitation.

Isabel's possible submission to external influence should
never, in the light of that passivity which we have seen to be
an essential component of her maintained independence, come
as a shock, nor should her seeming denial of it in her assertion
of self-control and self-knowledge, for the two contradictory
impulses concomitantly held are the mainstay of her notion of
the self. And that Isabel should at this time be acutely tuned
to contraries is largely the result of her having encountered in
Madame Merle, whom Ralph will call "the great round world
itself" (NY, III:362), the evident fulfilment of her own aspiration, a felt continuity between the self and the world. "Madame Merle liked almost everything," Isabel observes, and again:
"she appeared to have in her experience a touchstone for everything" (NY, III:269, 271). It is this inclusiveness—copious

enough, the girl feels, to embrace even the angularity of Henrietta Stackpole—which presents Isabel a model to be lived up to.

But if Madame Merle represents for Isabel the concretion of her own ideal, such a concretion must of necessity embody the paradoxes and antitheses, of which Isabel is only vaguely aware, implicit in the ideal. For if Isabel finds the talents, accomplishments; and aptitudes of Madame Merle suitable objects for emulation, she also finds them "enclosed," the fine flowers of a private garden from which she is strangely excluded. The sense of enclosure and of her own exclusion is in part, of course, Isabel's way of expressing her own distance from the accomplishments of Madame Merle; but it is also a suggestion of Madame Merle's finitude, of fixed limits imposed upon her attributes, a finitude at variance with the near-universality with which at other times her young friend invests her.

Shortly after, Isabel considers the older woman in the following way:

> She was never idle. . . . And with all this she had always the social quality, was never rudely absent and yet never too seated. . . . If for Isabel she had a fault it was that she was not natural; by which the girl meant, not that she was either affected or pretentious, since from these vulgar vices no woman could have been more exempt, but that her nature had been too much overlaid by custom and her angles too much rubbed away. She had become too flexible, too useful, was too ripe and too final. She was in a word too perfectly the social animal that man and woman are supposed to have been intended to be. . . . Isabel found it difficult to think of her in any detachment or privacy, she existed only in her relations, direct or indirect, with her fellow mortals. (NY, III:273–274)

The quality of paradox permeates Isabel's meditation, but it is paradox reduced almost to decorum and the mediation between antitheses, Madame Merle's seemingly constant activity counterbalanced, as it is, for Isabel by her "social quality," and that quality itself a balance between lack of inattention and lack of avidity, definable, in fact, only in a resolution of negatives.

Such a delicate tension between opposites is the achieved perfection which Isabel envies in Madame Merle, but it carries with it its own dangers. For in Madame Merle's social quality, in that flexibility which is the opposite of Isabel's own bemoaned lack of pliability, the girl detects a loss of the self in the relations into which it enters. Madame Merle is neither affected nor pretentious, for the appearance she presents to the world is not, to Isabel's mind, a false front masking her true self. Rather, the angularity of her individuality has been blunted by the social intercourse and custom with which she has been "overlaid" and which has become in fact her reality.

Madame Merle's usefulness, in which Isabel might well but does not detect the obverse ability to use, suggests a passive sense of life rather than a creative one—a suggestion underlined by her telling Isabel, "I want to see what life makes of you" (NY, III:268), and if passivity is a necessary implication of Isabel's ideal, it is not part of that ideal as projected. Madame Merle's ripeness and finality suggest a fulfilment which is at the same time a termination, the stasis of limit imposed upon even while it realizes potential. Madame Merle's perfection as the social animal is in some ways the achievement of what Henry James, Sr., saw as the perfection of the human condition, but her achievement is at the expense of what Isabel sees as her natural self. She seems to exist only in her relations—her self appears but the function of those relations. At this early stage in their acquaintance, Madame Merle comes, at her most portentous, to figure for Isabel as the symbol of that theory of internal relation for which the former severely argues, though personal relation rather than appurtenance determines her identity. If she is the fulfilment of an ideal, she is at the same time the fulfilment of its antithesis, and a subtle warning that the ideal's concretion may entail the generation of its antithesis.

Among Isabel's considerations of her friend's nature occurs a passage which reviews and develops some of the key terms of the novel and which advances the progression of paradox we have noted in the relation of Isabel to Madame Merle. In the original 1881 edition the passage reads:

Emotion, it is true, had become with her rather historic; she
made no secret of the fact that the fountain of sentiment,
thanks to having been rather violently tapped at one period,
did not flow quite so freely as of yore. Her pleasure now was
to judge rather than to feel; she freely admitted that of old
she had been rather foolish, and now she pretended to be wise.

"I judge more than I used to," she said to Isabel; "but it
seems to me that I have earned the right. One can't judge till
one is forty; before that we are too eager, too hard, too cruel,
and in addition too ignorant. I am sorry for you; it will be a
long time before you are forty. But every gain is a loss of some
kind; I often think that after forty one can't really feel. The
freshness, the quickness have certainly gone. You will keep
them longer than most people; it will be a great satisfaction
to me to see you some years hence. I want to see what life
makes of you. One thing is certain—it can't spoil you. It may
pull you about horribly; but I defy it to break you up." (PL,
163–164)

Madame Merle's pronouncement is essentially the same in the
New York Edition, but the sentence introducing it has been
interestingly changed:

She proposed moreover, as well as expected, to cease feeling;
she freely admitted that of old she had been a little mad, and
now she pretended to be perfectly sane. (NY, III:268)

In the revision the contrast of judgement and feeling has been
softened; they are no longer presented as mutually exclusive
terms (and James has improved the passage stylistically by re-
serving the word *judge* for the beginning of Madame Merle's
speech). At the same time, the substitution of "a little mad"
for "rather foolish" renders more thoroughly Madame Merle's
tone and replaces the concept of wisdom with that of sanity,
which is more in accord with the urbanity of what she is saying.
The word *pretended*, retained in the New York Edition, indicates at one level merely that Isabel suspects her friend still
capable of that passion which her pronouncement is meant to
deny, but at another that there is something sham about the
code which Madame Merle professes, denying as it does those
feelings which are the spontaneous hallmarks of the aspiring

self (a view in line with Isabel's later reflection that Madame
Merle is not natural, though neither affected nor pretentious).

But the main emphasis of the passage, as the beginning
of the subsequent paragraph points up—"Isabel received this
assurance as a young soldier, still panting from a slight skirmish
in which he has come off with honour, might receive a pat on
the shoulder from his colonel" (NY, III:268)—is the force of
her rather jaded compatriot's words on the mind of the impres-
sionable young girl. She regards her recent abstentions from
judgement under the guise of judgement as preservations of her
feelings (or perhaps, in the strain of Madame Merle's argu-
ments, as occasions when the self has successfully met the test
of feeling), even though her choice has been against attaching
her feelings to a particular object.

In effect, Madame Merle's disquisition on judgement and
feeling, though it begins as a paean to that judgement which
comes only subsequent to feeling's atrophy, is taken by Isabel
as a tribute to the splendor of her individuality and freedom,
which has just survived the buffets of two marriage proposals.
If by Madame Merle's theory she, whose sense of herself as a
judge is so mixed, is denied the ability to judge, she is at least
vouchsafed the integrity of feeling for which judgement must
provide a rather unsatisfactory alternative. For Madame Merle's
central thrust, despite its mild qualification in the revision,
is ultimately the either-or proposition that the ability to judge,
to make choices, distinctions, commitments in the realm of the
tangible—and this from the woman who for Isabel is nearly
universal in the realization of her taste—is necessarily preclusive
of the ability to feel and largely the result of that ability's decline, a decline not self-willed but imposed from without, from
the bruises which one has sustained in one's encounters with
the world, themselves perhaps having originated in feeling. Feeling has itself, in Madame Merle's version, been commitment
to the phenomenal, commitment rebounding in the destruction
of that very feeling and terminating in one's being left finally
with the exclusively phenomenal mode of operation which is
judgement.

Madame Merle's speech and Isabel's response to it are at once revealing and perplexing in the light of an earlier conversation between Isabel and her cousin:

> "You want to see life—you'll be hanged if you don't, as the young men say."
> "I don't think I want to see it as the young men want to see it. But I do want to look about me."
> "You want to drain the cup of experience."
> "No, I don't want to touch the cup of experience. It's a poisoned drink! I only want to see for myself."
> "You want to see, but not to feel," Ralph remarked.
> "I don't think that if one's a sentient being one can make the distinction." (NY, III:213)

Ralph's first comments exemplify again his tendency to see Isabel as he wants to, but his terminal accusation (or is it only a gloss?), though it is in part a device to draw Isabel out, has also in part its own justice, as Isabel's comment on the cup of experience indicates. That comment is of course motivated by her desire to preserve her freedom, which would be destroyed by the commitment to particularity which the cup of experience symbolizes for her. But Ralph is to a degree right, if not entirely serious, in accusing Isabel of a certain lack of feeling (a lack which many commentators háve been all too zealous in pointing out), for feeling is both the expression of individuality and the limiting condition of a relation established with someone or something external to oneself. Hence, though Isabel views the capacity for feeling as inextricable from the capacity for seeing—a capacity we have earlier noted as an imagination fundamentally antithetical to the faculty of judgement —there is in her a disjunction between the two, even if both are necessary components of her concept of the self. Seeing is the passive holding in tension of the self's possibilities; feeling is the projection of the self into the realm of existence, where limits are imposed upon it. The integrity of the self is the integral relation of seeing and feeling, but the destruction of that integrity is inherent in the necessity of feeling's attachment to what is not the self. The paradox is like that of self-expression, which is both manifestation and denial of the self: the mode of seeing implies the mode of feeling; but the mode of feeling entails that of judgement, which is the denial of the total potential implicit in the original vision.

VII

Such, then, are the paradoxes surrounding Isabel—paradoxes engendered by her own conception of herself and extended by the relations into which she has entered—when she becomes aware that her uncle has left her a sizeable fortune; and the fact of that inheritance will be the force which pushes them out of the tension of Isabel's imagination into the realm of action.

As we have already seen, Isabel's initial reaction to her inheritance, her withdrawal from the exercise of the power with which her money vests her, is explicable largely as a recoil from the commitment to particularity which such an exercise would imply. That note, which will become one of the primary burdens of her vigil by the fire, is strong in Chapter XX and in Chapter XXI, the two chapters which turn centrally on the question of her inheritance; but it is played against other strains, against appraisals from the other characters of the fortune's significance to Isabel.

Mrs. Touchett's view, for one, is characteristically worldly and unthinking:

> "Now that you're a young woman of fortune you must know how to play the part—I mean to play it well," she said to Isabel once for all; and she added that the girl's first duty was to have everything handsome. "You don't know how to take care of your things, but you must learn," she went on; this was Isabel's second duty. Isabel submitted, but for the present her imagination was not kindled; she longed for opportunities, but these were not the opportunities she meant. (NY, III:301–302)

Mrs. Touchett's imagination is entirely thing-oriented: Isabel is to surround herself with handsome things and devote herself to maintaining them. But the opportunities of possession are far from those of imaginative flight which Isabel has envisioned, and playing a part, assuming a fixed role, is wholly alien to her conception of herself.

A later statement of Mrs. Touchett's amplifies the ideas she has proposed and defines more clearly her notion of the freedom which wealth confers:

> "Now, of course, you're completely your own mistress and are as free as the bird on the bough. I don't mean you were not so before, but you're at present on a different footing— property erects a kind of barrier. You can do a great many things if you're rich which would be severely criticised if you were poor. You can go and come, you can travel alone, you can have your own establishment. . . . Of course you can do as you please; I only want you to understand how much you're at liberty." (NY, III:315)

Mrs. Touchett's idea of freedom is to be able to step into a series of social forms and positions which are denied those who lack the requisite wealth. It is, in essence, the ability to do certain things without being criticized for them, the ability that Mr. Touchett's money has presumably given his wife, though it has hardly caused all the other characters of the novel to refrain from criticizing her. But the terms in which Mrs. Touchett casts her idea of freedom are indeed strange: property "erects a kind of barrier" and thus imposes a limit upon the individual. Though this barrier protects the individual from outside attack, it negates the sense of continuity with the motions of the world which Isabel seeks: it insures a kind of freedom only at the price of that very isolation of which Isabel more and more senses Mrs. Touchett, amid her protestations of personal freedom, to be the victim. It is an envelope of circumstances, non-expressive and totally enclosing; and in what has become of Mrs. Touchett we see one of the extreme possibilities of what Isabel's freedom may ultimately amount to.[23]

On the other side of the coin we find Henrietta, the avowed opponent of Isabel's inheritance. Normally it is difficult

to regard Henrietta as anything like an intellectual center of
the novel, but in this case her lengthy admonition does register
some telling strokes against Isabel, qualified though the whole
speech may be by her preposterous references to "our western
cities" (In fact, one of James's techniques in this section of the
novel, in which Isabel is becoming attracted to Osmond, is to
put in the mouths of the secondary characters criticisms of Isabel and Osmond which are valid, if beside the point of Isabel's
basic dilemma.)

> "If Mr. Touchett had consulted me about leaving you the
> money," she frankly asserted, "I'd have said to him 'Never!' "
> "I see," Isabel had answered. "You think it will prove a
> curse in disguise. Perhaps it will."
> "Leave it to someone you care less for—that's what I
> should have said."
> . . . "Do you really believe it will ruin me?" . . .
> "I hope it won't ruin you; but it will certainly confirm
> your dangerous tendencies."
> "Do you mean the love of luxury—of extravagance?"
> "No, no," said Henrietta; "I mean your exposure on the
> moral side. I approve of luxury; I think we ought to be as
> elegant as possible. Look at the luxury of our western cities;
> I've seen nothing over here to compare with it. I hope you'll
> never become grossly sensual; but I'm not afraid of that. The
> peril for you is that you live too much in the world of your
> own dreams. You're not enough in contact with reality—with
> the toiling, striving, suffering, I may even say sinning, world
> that surrounds you. You're too fastidious; you've too many
> graceful illusions. Your newly-acquired thousands will shut you
> up more and more to the society of a few selfish and heartless
> people who will be interested in keeping them up."
> Isabel's eyes expanded as she gazed at this lurid scene.
> "What are my illusions?" she asked, "I try so hard not to have
> any."
> "Well," said Henrietta, "you think you can lead a ro-
> mantic life, that you can live by pleasing yourself and pleasing
> others. You'll find you're mistaken. Whatever life you lead you
> must put your soul in it—to make any sort of success of it;
> and from the moment you do that it ceases to be romance, I
> assure you: it becomes grim reality! And you can't always
> please yourself; you must sometimes please other people. That,

I admit, you're very ready to do; but there's another thing that's still more important—you must often *displease* others. You must always be ready for that—you must never shrink from it. That doesn't suit you at all—you're too fond of admiration, you like to be thought well of. You think we can escape disagreeable duties by taking romantic views—that's your great illusion, my dear. But we can't. You must be prepared on many occasions in life to please no one at all—not even yourself." (NY, III:309–311)

Henrietta's warning that Isabel will be shut up by her thousands underscores the portentous note in what Mrs. Touchett has said of property as a barrier (and, of course, points to Isabel's virtual imprisonment in Palazzo Roccanera by the ultimately selfish Osmond), and her mention of keeping up illusions recalls what Mrs. Touchett has seen as Isabel's second duty and suggests the identification of "things" and illusions.

More important, however, is Henrietta's attack on Isabel's romanticism, on her desire to please herself and everyone else at the same time. Such an attack may seem strange when levied at a girl who has just thoroughly displeased two importunate suitors, but it is an adequate reflection of Isabel's vision of herself as rendering a minimum of pain, as finding in herself a total accord with the rest of the world and expanding so as to embrace the world without drawing lines of demarcation which limit and exclude. Henrietta, in effect, sees Isabel's money as an encrustation which will seal her up even more thoroughly in the chambers of her romantic imagination and protect her from propulsion into the active world of reality. Henrietta's view of reality, it must be admitted, is a severely limited one, but her admonition does suggest what Isabel will actually do in her most significant attempt to preserve her freedom, when she makes her fortune over to Gilbert Osmond.

VIII

That what money confers, the ability to manifest freedom in concrete action rather than merely to preserve it in suspension, causes a certain fear in Isabel is underlined in a slightly later conversation with Ralph:

> "I try to care more about the world than about myself— but I always come back to myself. It's because I'm afraid." She stopped; her voice had trembled a little. "Yes, I'm afraid; I can't tell you. A large fortune means freedom, and I'm afraid of that. It's such a fine thing, and one should make such a good use of it. If one should n't one would be ashamed. And one must keep thinking; it's a constant effort. I'm not sure it's not a greater happiness to be powerless."
>
> "For weak people I've no doubt it's a greater happiness. For weak people the effort not to be contemptible must be. great."
>
> "And how do you know I'm not weak?" Isabel asked.
>
> "Ah," Ralph answered with a flush that the girl noticed, "if you are I'm awfully sold!" (NY, III:320)

Isabel's reflection on the happiness of powerlessness carries one back to her reception of the news that she has inherited a fortune and her lack of eagerness to take advantage of the power, the ability "to do," which the money has given her, and emphasizes the fact that although the money was presented in the spirit of liberation, it is received as a burden and impingement, even if the burden is just that of her freedom's extension. Her trying to care for the world more than herself and her inevitable return to herself are simply her desire for continuity—the idealistic inclusive extension of the self which imperils the self's identity in its very extension and which rebounds to a perilous self-preservation in passivity and powerlessness.

By the next page of the novel, however, Isabel has negotiated one of those rather stunning about-faces and has seemingly come quite to terms with her burden:

> She had at any rate before leaving San Remo grown used to feeling rich. The consciousness in question found a proper place in rather a dense little group of ideas that she had about herself, and often it was by no means the least agreeable. It took perpetually for granted a thousand good intentions. She lost herself in a maze of visions; the fine things to be done by a rich, independent, generous girl who took a large human

view of occasions and obligations were sublime in the mass.
Her fortune therefore became to her mind a part of her better
self; it gave her importance, gave her even, to her imagination,
a certain ideal beauty. (NY, III:321–322)

The conversion seems a thorough one; Isabel has, in effect,
imaginatively assimilated the money and made it "part of her
. . . self," regarding it no longer as an external appurtenance but
as a fact of her identity, an extension of her best qualities and a
stamp upon them. (That she considers the money to have *given*
her importance and a "certain ideal beauty" perhaps suggests
her sense of having originally lacked these qualities and indicates the extent of her capacity for moment-to-moment self-
delusion, though more likely it means that these inherent qualities of hers are filled out and blazoned to the world by her
inheritance.)

But that the actual money is still a burden to Isabel and
that only as a dimension of her imagination can she cope with
it are strongly pointed by the indefiniteness of "the fine things
to be done," the vagueness of her taking for granted "a thousand good intentions," and the "maze of visions" in which she
is in fact lost. She is soaring again, but her money will keep her
aloft only so long as its power is visionary and not the power
which must manifest itself in the actuality of choice. For this
brief time, however, the fusion of inheritance and imagination
is so successful that in the same paragraph we find her thinking
that "she had not given her last shilling, sentimentally speaking, either to Caspar Goodwood or to Lord Warburton, and yet
could n't but feel them appreciably in debt to her" (NY, III:
322)—conceiving the facts of her emotional life in rather brute
cash terms. These terms will ring more sinisterly later when
she compares the passion which she will supposedly bring Gilbert Osmond to a sum in the bank.

Of Isabel's dilemma, C. B. Cox says: "Above all, her idea
of freedom is a product of her romantic imagination and she is
afraid to apply herself to reality. This comes out not only in her
fear of sex, but also in her attitude to Mr. Touchett's legacy.

She is unequal to the responsibility. . . . To escape from the burden of free choice, Isabel allows herself to be seduced by the glitter of Osmond's sophistication."[24] Cox is one of the few critics to perceive that free choice is in some sense the burden which the fortune confers upon Isabel and to note that her choice of Osmond is in large measure an attempt to sidestep the real matter of choice altogether. But he does not cite the important fact that Isabel's attempt to avoid free choice is at the same time an attempt to preserve freedom, and his treatment of the reasons for her accepting Osmond is rather scanty. Those reasons—a complex of ideas bound up with Isabel's concepts of freedom and externals, as developed in her confrontations with her two former suitors, with Madame Merle, and with her fortune—must concern us here.

IX

The question of Osmond's identity—or, in the worldly sense, his lack of one—is paramount in the early stages of his presentation and is largely determinant of Isabel's eventual choice. Madame Merle, when she first broaches the subject of Osmond to Isabel, denigrates him in such a fashion that he is sure to be a figure of interest to the girl. Madame Merle begins by questioning the identity of Ralph Touchett, proceeds by subsuming that of his father under her own theory of externals, and concludes by producing Osmond as the extreme of Ralph's case, the man who has no external accomplishment or position to show for himself:

> "Look at poor Ralph Touchett: what sort of a figure do you call that? Fortunately he has a consumption; I say fortunately, because it gives him something to do. His consumption's his *carrière*; it's a kind of position. . . . But without that who would he be, what would he represent? 'Mr. Ralph Touchett: an American who lives in Europe.' That signifies absolutely nothing—it's impossible anything should signify less. . . . With the poor old father it's different; he has his identity, and it's rather a massive one. He represents a great financial house,

and that, in our day, is as good as anything else. . . . The worst case, I think, is a friend of mine, a countryman of ours, who lives in Italy (where he also was brought before he knew better), and who is one of the most delightful men I know. . . . I'll bring you together and then you'll see what I mean. He's Gilbert Osmond—he lives in Italy; that's all one can say about him or make of him. He's exceedingly clever, a man made to be distinguished; but, as I tell you, you exhaust the description when you say he's Mr. Osmond who lives *tout bêtement* in Italy. No career, no name, no position, no fortune, no past, no future, no anything." (NY, III:280–281)

Madame Merle is of course extremely conscious of the repugnance which Isabel has shown for her theory of identity, as expressed in their earlier "metaphysical" discussion, and her attack on Ralph's "position" is a calculated device which can only strengthen Isabel's affection for her cousin. When she questions what Ralph "represents" and asserts what Mr. Touchett does, she is flying in the face of Isabel's own cherished notions of a self which not only does not represent something other than itself but also cannot itself be represented— and she is, of course, if unknowingly, looking forward to the time when Isabel will be called upon to "represent" Osmond.

To introduce at this point the figure of Gilbert Osmond is a masterstroke on Madame Merle's part, since he becomes associated with the autonomous individual, becomes even the epitome of it. His lack of external determination and definition— the fact that he lacks career, name, position, fortune, past, future, anything, that he is, in short, the antithesis of everything that Lord Warburton is—is what will appeal to Isabel, what will make him figure for her the free individual unconstrained by externals.[25] Why, then, Osmond will not do for Isabel's advisers, or even for his own sister (NY, III:391–392), is precisely why he *will* do for Isabel. Her acceptance of him is no mere perverse refusal to abide by the counsel which she receives—though that does enter in her desire to act only as herself—but the necessary working out of the theory of herself which she entertains.

That Madame Merle's subtle effort has not been in vain is frequently attested by Isabel's assertions of Osmond's merits, particularly on those occasions, also frequent, when she is called upon to defend him. Among her clustered impressions upon the occasion of her first seeing Osmond in his own surroundings is the following:

> His pictures, his medallions and tapestries were interesting; but after a while Isabel felt the owner much more so, and independently of them, thickly as they seemed to overhang him. He resembled no one she had ever seen; most of the people she knew might be divided into groups of half a dozen specimens. . . . Her mind contained no class offering a natural place to Mr. Osmond—he was a specimen apart. (NY, III:375–376)

What she has heard of Osmond from Madame Merle and what she feels of his charm in his presence separate him for her from his appurtenances, give him an identity which may perhaps express itself in the perfect taste with which he has surrounded himself but which is free of essential definition by those surroundings. The fact that she has never before met anyone like him renders him for her a specimen apart, someone not to be categorized and classified but to be accepted on the merits of his own distinct individuality.

Somewhat later in the same scene, Isabel, as is her wont, misses the warning note in what Osmond gives her and, just as Ralph has done with her, fills him out along the lines of her own consciousness:

> "I don't mean to say I've cared for nothing; but the things I've cared for have been definite—limited. The events of my life have been absolutely unperceived by any one save myself; getting an old silver crucifix at a bargain (I've never bought anything dear, of course), or discovering, as I once did, a sketch by Correggio on a panel daubed over by some inspired idiot."
> This would have been rather a dry account of Mr. Osmond's career if Isabel had fully believed it; but her imagination supplied the human element which she was sure had not been wanting. His life had been mingled with other lives

more than he admitted. . . . It was her present inclination, however, to express a measured sympathy for the success with which he had preserved his independence. "That's a very pleasant life," she said, "to renounce everything but Correggio!"

"Oh, I've made in my way a good thing of it. Don't imagine I'm whining about it. It's one's own fault if one isn't happy."

This was large; she kept down to something smaller. (NY, III:382–383)

What Osmond, in effect, presents to Isabel is the finitude of his achievement—a finitude, however, which she will flood and magnanimously distort by the lights of her own imagination. The dryness is indeed there, though not so much in the account as in that consciousness whose career it sketches, and the crowning irony lies in Osmond's total lack of that "human element" which Isabel readily supplies and in the particular nature, the details of which the Countess Gemini will finally reveal to her, of his life's mingling with those of others.

But if the "definite," the "limited," the renunciation of "everything but Correggio" strike a note totally at variance with Isabel's own design, they can attest, for her at this point sufficiently generous mind, the preservation, under externally imposed limit, of a fine independence, a selectivity operative as discriminating expressiveness. Unconsciously, for Isabel, the appeal of Osmond's renunciation is its echo of her own flight from choice in the world, though the "definite," the "limited," the excluding preference for Correggio prefigure the adjustment of her system which Isabel will make in the early stages of the second volume and even—in association then with a qualified idea of renunciation—the aspect her vision will take in the novel's final pages. All this, however, is merely underlying and foreshadowing. The conscious appeal for Isabel now is the small but intense romance of "getting an old silver crucifix at a bargain" and the implied possibility (Osmond is almost vulgarly insistent about how hard up he is) of what such an independence might do were it given a fortune the size of Isabel's with which to operate.

Isabel's belief in Osmond's individuality and independence
—those qualities which, as we shall see, she throws in the face
of her relations on the question of Osmond—runs strong in her
meditations after he has presented himself at the Palazzo
Crescentini:

> Mr. Osmond's talk was not injured by the indication of an
> eagerness to shine; Isabel found no difficulty in believing that
> a person was sincere who had so many of the signs of strong
> conviction—as for instance an explicit and graceful apprecia-
> tion of anything that might be said on his own side of the
> question, said perhaps by Miss Archer in especial. What con-
> tinued to please this young woman was that while he talked
> so for amusement he did n't talk, as she had heard people,
> for "effect." He uttered his ideas as if, odd as they often ap-
> peared, he were used to them and had lived with them; old
> polished knobs and heads and handles, of precious substance,
> that could be fitted if necessary to new walking-sticks—not
> switches plucked in destitution from the common tree and
> and then too elegantly waved about. (NY, III:400)[26]

Osmond's originality is evident for Isabel in the very oddness
of his ideas. His "eagerness to shine" is not a false front created
for "effect" to impress the world, but a true externalization of
his individuality, differentiated in its alternation of diffidence
and aggressiveness from the too perfect manner of Madame
Merle—a conduct not determined by those to whom it is ad-
dressed and inculpable particularly when Isabel is its object.
Matter and manner are perfectly aligned—there is for Isabel in
Osmond that much desired continuity of the inner and the externalization, with none of the ostentatious brandishing of twigs
from the tree of common saws which signals both the breakdown of continuity and the absence of originality and, hence,
of freedom. Osmond, in lacking an envelope of circumstances,
is able to externalize himself perfectly—or at least that is the
way Isabel views the case.

The image which depicts Osmond's ideas for Isabel, however, may catch us up short, suggesting as it does Osmond's
aestheticism, that "sterile" dilettantism of which Ralph will
accuse him (NY, IV:71), and preparing for the sinister passage

at the beginning of Volume II in which Osmond senses Isabel "as smooth to his general need of her as handled ivory to the palm" (NY, IV:11). Whether or not Isabel has already been tainted by Osmond's aestheticism (Powers's view of her as an Osmondian acquisitor would have this an incipient trait), she misses the implicit warning in her own metaphor, figuring with it only the beauty of Osmond's externalizing his original, his independent self.[27]

"I've too little to offer you. What I have—it's enough for me; but it's not enough for you. I've neither fortune, nor fame, nor extrinsic advantages of any kind. So I offer nothing" (NY, IV:18). So Osmond proposes to Isabel, neglecting to add that fortune, fame, and extrinsic advantages are precisely what he hopes to gain by his suit—and so will Isabel's friends and relations, in the three major confrontations at the beginning of the second volume, argue against her accepting his proposal and throw her back on the basic premise of his intrinsicalness.

Caspar Goodwood, after his hurried descent on Rome, precipitated by Isabel's announcement of her engagement, is the first to put Isabel through the mill, and his interrogation begins on the question of Henrietta Stackpole's knowledge of Osmond:

> "Does she know Mr. Osmond?" he enquired.
> "A little. And does n't like him. But of course I don't marry to please Henrietta," she added.
> . . . "Is it a marriage your friends won't like?" he demanded.
> "I really have n't an idea. As I say, I don't marry for my friends."
> . . . "Who and what then is Mr. Gilbert Osmond?"
> "Who and what? Nobody and nothing but a very good and very honourable man. He's not in business," said Isabel. "He's not rich; he's not known for anything in particular."
> . . . "Where does he come from? Where does he belong?"
> . . . "He comes from nowhere. He has spent most of his life in Italy."
> "You said in your letter he was American. Has n't he a native place?"
> "Yes, but he has forgotten it. He left it as a small boy."

"Has he never gone back?"

"Why should he go back?" Isabel asked, flushing all defensively. "He has no profession."

"He might have gone back for pleasure. Does n't he like the United States?"

"He does n't know them. Then he's very quiet and very simple—he contents himself with Italy."

"With Italy and with you," said Mr. Goodwood with gloomy plainness and no appearance of trying to make an epigram. "What has he ever done?" he added abruptly.

"That I should marry him? Nothing at all," Isabel replied while her patience helped itself by turning a little to hardness. "If he had done great things would you forgive me any better? Give me up, Mr. Goodwood; I'm marrying a perfect nonentity. Don't try to take an interest in him. You can't."

"I can't appreciate him; that's what you mean. And you don't mean in the least that he's a perfect nonentity. You think he's grand, you think he's great, though no one else thinks so."

"Why do you always come back to what others think? I can't discuss Mr. Osmond with you." (NY, IV:46–48)

The two basic strains of Isabel's defense of her choice of Osmond are her own independence ("I don't marry to please Henrietta," "I don't marry for my friends," "Why do you always come back to what others think?"—the primary irony of this challenge being that it is Osmond, more than any other character, who inevitably comes back to what others think) and Osmond's intrinsicalness, almost a corollary, for her, of his lacking an external context. Osmond is "nobody and nothing" in the world's terms. He cannot be placed and positioned; he is only "a very good and very honourable man," and Isabel bitingly hastens to add that "He's not in business," as if his being so would automatically preclude goodness and honor, though, as we have seen, she does not, in her less agitated moments, accuse Goodwood of a commercial avidity. Osmond's not being rich is both the lack of an envelope of circumstances and the temptation to provide him with one, his not being known for anything in particular both the escape from fixity and the appeal of the general. His coming from nowhere implies, in the context of Goodwood's associated question, that he belongs anywhere and everywhere, though "he contents himself with Italy" just as he has contented himself with Correggio. If he comes originally from America, the fact is not a defining one (as it is, say, for Henrietta); if he lives in Italy, the fact does not exclude his other potentialities. He is not defined by, but rather capable of relationship with, whatever environment he is in. His having done nothing, his being a perfect nonentity is the sign for her of his integrity, and Goodwood rightly translates what she has said from the world's terms into her own.

Mrs. Touchett, in the following chapter, raises some of the same objections:

> . . . "You're going to marry that man."
>
> "What man do you mean?" Isabel inquired with great dignity.
>
> "Madame Merle's friend—Mr. Osmond."
>
> "I don't know why you call him Madame Merle's friend. Is that the principal thing he's known by?"
>
> "If he's not her friend he ought to be—after what she has done for him!" cried Mrs. Touchett. . . . "Was it for this that you refused Lord Warburton?"
>
> "Please don't go back to that. Why should n't I like Mr. Osmond, since others have done so?"
>
> "Others, at their wildest moments, never wanted to marry him. There's nothing of him," Mrs. Touchett explained.
>
> "Then he can't hurt me," said Isabel. . . .
>
> "People usually marry as they go into partnership—to set up a house. But in your partnership you'll bring everything."
>
> "Is it that Mr. Osmond is n't rich? Is that what you're talking about?" Isabel asked.
>
> "He has no money; he has no name; he has no importance. I value such things and I have the courage to say it; I think they're very precious. Many other people think the same, and they show it. But they give some other reason."
>
> Isabel hesitated a little. "I think I value everything that's valuable. I care very much for money, and that's why I wish Mr. Osmond to have a little."
>
> "Give it to him then; but marry some one else."

"His name is good enough for me," the girl went on. "It's a very pretty name. Have I such a fine one myself?" (NY, IV:53–55)

Isabel's defense of Osmond to Mrs. Touchett (whose attack is virtually a recapitulation of Madame Merle's catalogue of Osmond's deficiencies), in addition to reiterating points already made to Goodwood, takes some new and rather perverse directions. Her reaction to Mrs. Touchett's referring to him as "Madame Merle's friend," for example, is almost unnaturally defensive and insists too fiercely on Osmond's intrinsic merit. He is certainly and publicly a friend of Madame Merle's, and there is no denigration necessarily implied in his being referred to as such, though Isabel's vehemence does indeed provoke Mrs. Touchett immediately to strike a portentous note. Similarly, it is rather strange for the Isabel who protests that she does not marry for others to cite among Osmond's credentials the fact that "others" have liked him, though Isabel with her back to the wall, as she apparently finds herself now, is inclined to grasp at inconsequent straws. The fact that she is primarily parrying Mrs. Touchett's thrusts rather than seriously arguing her case becomes evident in her seemingly irrelevant though ironically significant reply to Mrs. Touchett's charge that there is "nothing of him"—a charge which, in the basically commercial twist Isabel's aunt then gives it, echoes those levied against Osmond by both Goodwood and the Countess.

When the question of Osmond's "name" comes up, Isabel's wit sufficiently indicates the view which she takes of the external. At the same time, though, she strikes the note which, in the colloquy with Madame Merle prior to her inheritance, and later in her own coming to terms with that fact, she has already sounded. She asserts, that is, her own high, if unclear, valuation of money in terms which suggest the continuity between herself and the rest of the world—the identity of those things intrinsically valuable with those things which she herself values. Thus she indicates within the space of a few lines her two familiarly contradictory attitudes toward the self's relation to the rest of the world.

Ralph Touchett, who elicits Isabel's final defense of her husband-to-be, is Osmond's most serious and important critic, though his criticism, unfortunately for Isabel, utilizes at least in part the terms which she has become accustomed to hear from the Countess Gemini, Goodwood, and Mrs. Touchett. To Ralph's demurral that "I did n't think you'd decide for—well, for *that* type," Isabel's predictable response is: "What's the matter with Mr. Osmond's type, if it be one? His being so independent, so individual, is what *I* most see in him" (NY, IV:68). Part of Osmond's fascination for her, as we have seen, is that he defies being typed. But his supposed independence and individuality, traits which she values supremely as characterizing herself, are actually figments of her imagination, formed out of his very lack of externals—so that his identity for her is paradoxically constituted by a negative envelope of circumstances—rather than realities of his being.[28]

Ralph's next objection reiterates a worldly point already made by her other advisers, and she is quick to dispose of it in the terms most characteristically her own:

> "I believed you'd marry a man of more importance."
> Cold, I say, her tone had been, but at this a colour like a flame leaped into her face. "Of more importance to whom? It seems to me enough that one's husband should be of importance to one's self!" (NY, IV:68–69)

One of James's most telling strokes here is to have made Isabel's retort virtually unanswerable, even if her defense does go hopelessly askew of its object. Ralph's charge, as couched (though not as meant), is certainly a rather cheap, worldly commonplace. (To accept its merits as a generalization would be more or less to accept the view that Isabel should have married someone with a superior position, and clearly the *Portrait* does not deal in simplicities of this variety.) Isabel's rebuttal is therefore one with which every reader can at least superficially agree. Its flaw is that surfaces, in this case surfaces which Isabel has unknowingly collaborated with Osmond in creating, will ultimately count little for her—that, no matter how general the validity of her assertion, it is undercut by her having valued what is not in itself valuable.

The extent of Isabel's misreading of Osmond becomes fully apparent several pages later as she continues to dilate on the matter of his "importance":

> "I can't enter into your idea of Mr. Osmond; I can't do it justice, because I see him in quite another way. He's not important—no, he's not important; he's a man to whom importance is supremely indifferent. If that's what you mean when you call him 'small,' then he's as small as you please. I call that large—it's the largest thing I know." (NY, IV:72)

This is indeed wide of the mark as a description of the one man in all her world who covets external importance, but it is a natural consequence of her theory in action. Interesting as well are certain implications of Isabel's words, though the implications do not necessarily match her intent. Isabel seems, in denying her ability to enter into Ralph's idea of Osmond and to do it "justice," to accord his view its own private validity and to postulate that complete relativity of value which would be the consequence of her own idealism at its solipsistic extreme. Her subsequent comments seem to reinforce the point: what is "small" to Ralph is "large" to her; the linguistic formulation is irrelevant to the fact purportedly being described and is only an expression of opinion. Isabel sounds here like an early emotivist, though in fact she means only that Ralph's valuation is wrong and hers right. Nor is such an ambiguity intended by James, for the novel's value judgements hardly disappear in any agreement to disagree but remain fully open to argument and to the test of experience, which will prove the validity of Ralph's judgement to have been more than subjective. The significant point, nevertheless, is that, whatever meaning Isabel intends and no matter how clear that meaning is to the reader, her words betray the extreme workings out of that theory which has placed her where she can be so mistaken.

Within the same speech Isabel continues to outline, in a familiar vein, Osmond's virtues and the opportunity which her fortune presents her, concluding on what it should be sufficiently clear is the chief constituent of his attraction for her—his lack of appurtenances, his being the total antithesis to what Lord Warburton represented for her:

> "Pray, would you wish me to make a mercenary marriage—what they call a marriage of ambition? I've only one ambition —to be free to follow out a good feeling. I had others once, but they've passed away. Do you complain of Mr. Osmond because he's not rich? That's just what I like him for. I've fortunately money enough; I've never felt so thankful for it as to-day. There have been moments when I should like to go and kneel down by your father's grave: he did perhaps a better thing than he knew when he put it into my power to marry a poor man—a man who has borne his poverty with such dignity, with such indifference. Mr. Osmond has never scrambled nor struggled—he has cared for no worldly prize. If that's to be narrow, if that's to be selfish, then it's very well. I'm not frightened by such words, I'm not even displeased; I'm only sorry that you should make a mistake. . . . Your mother has never forgiven me for not having come to a better understanding with Lord Warburton, and she's horrified at my contenting myself with a person who has none of his great advantages—no property, no title, no honours, no houses, nor lands, nor position, nor reputation, nor brilliant belongings of any sort. It's the total absence of all these things that pleases me. Mr. Osmond's simply a very lonely, a very cultivated and a very honest man—he's not a prodigious proprietor." (NY, IV:73–74)

The linguistic issue Isabel simply sweeps aside: such words do not frighten her because Ralph is merely mistaken. But unwittingly she utters something perilously near the whole truth with her glib "That's just what I like him for" and "It's the total absence of all these things that pleases me." By marrying the man who is "not a prodigious proprietor" she can be relieved of the burden of herself being one, though the act will confer on both of them a measure of that dubious status which she has seen him lack and has herself fled. And to Ralph's troubled consciousness is left the summary of Isabel's deluded act of conversion, even though the springs of the delusion are not perfectly clear to him:

> She was wrong, but she believed; she was deluded, but she was dismally consistent. It was wonderfully characteristic of her that, having invented a fine theory about Gilbert Osmond, she loved him not for what he really possessed, but for his very poverties dressed out as honours. Ralph remembered what he had said to his father about wishing to put it into her power to meet the requirements of her imagination. He had done so, and the girl had taken full advantage of the luxury. Poor Ralph felt sick; he felt ashamed. (NY, IV:74–75)

x

If Ralph is struck with the consistency of Isabel's paradoxical position, the reader has by this point been struck with an inconsistency which is a further turn of the paradoxical screw, which represents a further development of Isabel's theory in action and accounts, whether as cause or justification, for her ability even to act to the extent of choosing Osmond, though that choice is one against choice, an act which obviates action. We have already noted Henrietta's comment on Isabel's desire to please everyone, and Isabel herself, at the beginning of her interview with Caspar Goodwood, is thinking, "What a pity too that one can't satisfy everybody!" (NY, IV:43). The desire for an inclusive gesture of gratification, a sign of the harmonious continuity of self with others, is still present; but the desire is undercut by her already made decision to accept Gilbert Osmond and thereby to delimit the possibilities of relationship open to her.

What Goodwood at this point receives, in place of the tenuous stringing-along which she has treated him to previously, is a clear-cut rejection (even though Isabel, in her later sorrow, will view him as the most pressing part of her "unfinished business"), and the relation with Goodwood is not the only one she sees as having broken down:

She married to please herself. One did other things to please other people; one did this for a more personal satisfaction. . . . The passion of love separated its victim terribly from every one but the loved object. She felt herself disjoined from every one she had ever known before—from her two sisters, . . . from Henrietta, who, she was sure, would come out, too late, on purpose to remonstrate; from Lord Warburton, who would certainly console himself, and from Caspar Goodwood, who perhaps would not; from her aunt, who had cold, shallow ideas about marriage, for which she was not sorry to display her contempt; and from Ralph, whose talk about having great views for her was surely but a whimsical cover for a personal disappointment. (NY, IV:77–78)

Isabel has at least in part realized the necessity of submitting to some circumscription, some limitation within which her aspiration may reach fruition—though her alienation from all her former friends might warn her of the danger in the particular circumscription she chooses—and portions of her conversation with Ralph serve to heighten for the reader her change:

"You must have changed immensely. A year ago you valued your liberty beyond everything. You wanted only to see life."

"I've seen it," said Isabel. "It does n't look to me now, I admit, such an inviting expanse."

"I don't pretend it is; only I had an idea that you took a genial view of it and wanted to survey the whole field."

"I've seen that one can't do anything so general. One must choose a corner and cultivate that." (NY, IV:65)

Isabel's professed opinion of "life" hearkens back to her protective mode of retreat, protective of that very liberty which Ralph now sees her as having renounced, and particularly to her description of the "poisoned" cup of experience, which she has shrunk from touching; and the final image of the corner which she chooses suggests not only the cultivation of Voltairean gardens but also the deepest shade of the figurative cage of those opportunities which Warburton offered her. More telling, even, is her rejection of anything so general as surveying "the whole field" and her settling for the particularity implied in her choice. She reinforces the point later in the same conversation: "You talk about one's soaring and sailing, but if one marries at all one touches the earth. One has human feelings and needs, one has a heart in one's bosom, and one must marry a particular individual" (NY, IV:74). The point as she states it is, granted, a little glimpse into the obvious, but it is nevertheless a radical departure from Isabel's habitual mode of eschewing the particular for the generality of "soaring and sailing."

The most significant delineation of Isabel's changed view comes, however, in the following chapter:

> The desire for unlimited expansion had been succeeded in her soul by the sense that life was vacant without some private duty that might gather one's energies to a point. She had told Ralph she had "seen life" in a year or two and that she was already tired, not of the act of living, but of that of observing. What had become of all her ardours, her aspirations, her theories, her high estimate of her independence and her incipient conviction that she should never marry? These things had been absorbed in a more primitive need—a need the answer to which brushed away numberless questions, yet gratified infinite desires. It simplified the situation at a stroke, it came down from above like the light of the stars, and it needed no explanation. There was explanation enough in the fact that he was her lover, her own, and that she should be able to be of use to him. She could surrender to him with a kind of humility, she could marry him with a kind of pride; she was not only taking, she was giving. (NY, IV:82)

What indeed, one might ask, has become of "all her ardours, her aspirations, her theories, her high estimate of her independence," if she is so content to allow her "desire for unlimited expansion" to pass from her and to settle for the commonplaces of particularity? The answer is not quite the one which Isabel herself gives, for it is not primarily a renunciation of her early aspirations, with that set of needs being replaced by another. Rather, those early aspirations are channeled into and realized in their own seeming renunciation.

In one sense Isabel has come to see that unlimited expansion is impossible, is in fact a contradiction of terms, beyond the level of sheer desire—that expansion, in terms of action and not just imaginative flight, imposes its own limits. But her renunciation of unlimited expansion is also dictated by that very drive toward expansion, is less a willed renunciation (though, ironically, it will prove to be a nonvolitional one) than a concretion of her aspirations in the particularity she chooses. Thus in her "private duty" all her energies will be gathered "to a point"; thus the simplification of her choice, gratifying, as she says it does, "infinite desires," can satisfy her taste for the unlimited.

Isabel's professed reasons for choosing Osmond all finally point to her regarding him as a kind of concrete universal—a particular individual who is yet free of determination by external context and who, in the fullness of his potentiality, functions for her as a surrogate independent self. Finally there is the matter of what Isabel can bring to Osmond, perhaps the most important factor of all in creating the seeming shift in her attitude. For, as we shall learn in the fireside vigil, it is her fortune itself which looms as the most ponderous limitation upon her independence; and her choice of Osmond, which she here figures as a renunciation of her old aspirations, is actually a measure taken to preserve those aspirations, that independence. That conferring her fortune upon Osmond may impinge upon the independence which she postulates in him and for which she values him, that he too might suffer under its weight, does not seem to strike Isabel. Even further from her mind is the ultimate sacrifice of her own independence which the gesture will entail.

XI

If such is Isabel's elaborately misguided sense of Osmond, Osmond's sense of her is virtually antithetical and accordingly simple. If he is for her a surrogate free self, the actualization of her flights and aspirations, she is for him a surrogate fixed self, the concrete representation of his taste. Whereas Ralph envisions Isabel in flight, in the realization of her potentialities, Osmond prefers to see her having been brought down to earth, in that very condition which Ralph, using the image of the faded rose, will describe her acceptance of Osmond as having brought about: "I don't want to see you on your travels. I'd rather see you when they're over. I should like to see you when you're tired and satiated. . . . I shall prefer you in that state" (NY, IV:14).

Osmond's preference is in effect for an Isabel jaded, weary of experience, not fulfilled but overfilled, satiated—an Isabel not unlike the one, very much of his own making, who near the end lies back passively in the railway carriage bearing her away from Rome (a carriage which inevitably recalls an earlier imaged one) and allows "the grey curtain of her indifference" to close her in. What Osmond sees in Isabel is not her self but simply his surrogate, the representation of her husband at the expense of her own autonomy: "His 'style' was what the girl had discovered with a little help; and now, beside herself enjoying it, she should publish it to the world without his having any of the trouble. She should do the thing for him, and he would not have waited in vain" (NY, IV:12).

That Isabel is little more than an object for Osmond becomes manifest in his later development of her ability to "publish" his "style":

> He was immensely pleased with his young lady; Madame Merle had made him a present of incalculable value. . . . What could be a happier gift in a companion than a quick, fanciful mind which saved one repetitions and reflected one's thought on a polished, elegant surface? . . . His egotism had never taken the crude form of desiring a dull wife; this lady's intelligence was to be a silver plate, not an earthen one. . . . He found the silver quality in this perfection in Isabel; he could tap her imagination with his knuckle and make it ring. He knew perfectly, though he had not been told, that their union enjoyed little favour with the girl's relations; but he had always treated her so completely as an independent person that it hardly

seemed necessary to express regret for the attitude of her family. (NY, IV:79–80)

Osmond's cynical reference to Isabel's "imagination" shows how far his sense of that faculty lies from hers, just as his conception of her independence extends only so far as her wealth and her lack of any ties which might hinder his suit.

Isabel's independence and imagination, the two key qualities in her self-analysis, are valuable to Osmond only insofar as they are of use to him. She is merely a collector's item, if a rare and precious one; and the value of a collector's item, for Osmond, lies not in its intrinsic beauty but in what it tells about the taste of the collector—particularly if the item is a human one and happens to have resisted being acquired by another, and materially magnificent, collector:

> We know that he was fond of originals, of rarities, of the superior and the exquisite; and now that he had seen Lord Warburton, whom he thought a very fine example of his race and order, he perceived a new attraction in the idea of taking to himself a young lady who had qualified herself to figure in his collection of choice objects by declining so noble a hand. Gilbert Osmond had a high appreciation of this particular patriciate; not so much for its distinction, which he thought easily surpassable, as for its solid actuality. . . . It would be proper that the woman he might marry should have done something of that sort. (NY, IV:9)

The "solid actuality" of the British nobility translates rather easily into cash and underscores strikingly the mercenary orientation of Osmond's brand of aestheticism. What is most striking, though, is of course his reduction of Isabel to the status of object—an objectification of consciousness totally at variance with Isabel's habit of converting objects into the stuff of imagination.

As we have seen, however, Isabel's converting imagination entails at the same time the threat for Osmond of that objective determination, and hence reification, which she fears for herself. In fact, her Osmondian tendency has begun by this time, whether as the necessary antithesis of her idealism or simply as the result of Osmond's influence, to show up vividly in her meditation, so that we find her, as she awaits her interview with Caspar Goodwood, feeling "older—ever so much, and as if she were 'worth more' for it, like some curious piece in an antiquary's collection" (NY, IV:42).[29] Her thoughts indeed project not a little that satiety which Osmond has wished for her—her world travels have in large part borne the desired fruit—and they are closely aligned with her shift into the mode of particularity, fraught with the universalizing drive though that seeming alteration may be. But they are at the same time a further extension of that passivity which we have seen all along as the dark underside of Isabel's idealistic imagination, the retreat from limiting activity which converts subject into object in the very attempt of permitting the inverse conversion.[30]

The same tendency appears in a somewhat earlier passage —immediately following Osmond's declaration of love—which imagistically compresses the multiple and contradictory aspects of Isabel's predicament as she moves toward her choice of Osmond:

> "Oh, don't say that, please," she answered with an intensity that expressed the dread of having, in this case too, to choose and decide. What made her dread great was precisely the force which, as it would seem, ought to have banished all dread— the sense of something within herself, deep down, that she supposed to be inspired and trustful passion. It was there like a large sum stored in a bank—which there was a terror in having to begin to spend. If she touched it, it would all come out. (NY, IV:18)

The reasons for her dread of having once again to choose and decide are by now established, as is that for her ultimately choosing Osmond—the former that passivity and reaction which attend the sense (hardly a formulated belief) that active choice limits total freedom, the latter the belief that Osmond is the ideal example of the free self unconstrained by externals. But beyond the sheer dread of choice with which Isabel faces all three proposals is the intensity of internal pressure which she feels on this occasion alone. The total expenditure of her "passion" seems to imply for her a collapse of selfhood, a Tristanesque annihilation of the *principium individuationis* (a principle basic to Isabel's sense of herself, even though it implies the concept of limit and hence denies the self as all-possibility), and a submission to a Romanticism at odds with her own.[31]

What signifies most prominently, though, is the image which Isabel employs to convey her passion.[32] With it she points to what her fireside meditation will reveal as the primary cause of her having chosen Osmond, the burden of that enormous fortune which Ralph has had his father bestow on her in order to ensure her freedom. But it is a characteristic paradox that the tenor for which Isabel employs such a vehicle is that very selfhood which bears the burden, for which the fortune provides a limiting and defining envelope of circumstance.

The vehicle, however, is significantly not cash in action but a "sum stored in a bank," the figurative extension of Isabel's earlier reflections, upon receiving her inheritance, concerning the ability "to do." In the earlier passage Isabel relishes the power which money confers, but she draws back from exercising it. The money is, in something like Ralph's sense, a surrogate for the potentialities of the self, which, however (and this only in Isabel's sense, not Ralph's), will destroy part of that potential. In the latter passage the figurative money functions in much the same way as a surrogate self. As long as it is in Isabel's emotional bank, it and she are safe. Once it is touched, however, the entire fortune is endangered; that is, in Isabel's absolutist terms, once any affective possibility is actualized, her very nature as a vessel of potential is altered and sacrificed. The giving of the part is the giving of the entirety, for the integrity of the whole perishes in the giving. In the earlier passage, conversion is from the material to the mental, the fortune seen in terms of imaginative potential. In the latter passage the conversion is seemingly the reverse, the potentials of the self seen in terms of the material fortune.

But the distinction is perhaps misleading, as is labelling the earlier fortune any less figurative than the latter. The money, in either case, whether tenor or vehicle, exists effectively in Isabel's imagination, where it enters into total poetic synthesis with the imagination's own concept of itself. Whether it has any literal existence (in the first case it does, in the second it does only tangentially) is irrelevant to its being a mental fact. It is only, however, in its idle condition, unspent, that money is imaginatively convertible. Thus one may say that, at least for Isabel, money exists imaginatively only when it does not exist literally, only when it is sheer potential, when it does not participate in movement, in events.

The novel presents, then, two senses of money: money as envelope of circumstances, operative within the realm of actuality, necessitating participation in events which limit the ideal self—the money Isabel marries Osmond to get rid of; and money as potential, as a fact of the imagination, nonoperative because existent only within the static realm of ideality, not limiting the ideal self because it is its coextensive and self-generated symbol. And the dark implication of her metaphor, unsensed by Isabel, is that to save the selfhood which she images as a sum in the bank, she will make over to the man whom she endows with the best taste in the world the literal sum itself. She will, that is, bequeath to Osmond its literality but preserve for herself, by that very gesture, its imaginative reality. The bestowal, however, will paradoxically emerge the unsought conversion of herself into the terms of externality, into the object of her malignant husband's use.

XII

The remainder of *The Portrait of a Lady* is concerned with the aftermath of Isabel's marriage to Gilbert Osmond, the revelation to Isabel of what she has let herself in for, and her confrontation of her dilemma. (The revelation itself occurs during the lapse of time between Chapters XXXV and XXXVI; and it is one of James's great strokes to present Isabel primarily from the outside during the last part of the novel until Chapter XLII, when we are given at once her sense of what has happened to her.) Her dilemma is, in brief, that her marriage has totally annihilated the desired continuity between herself and the rest of the world. It has effected a complete divorce of Isabel as she is from Isabel as she appears (the "portrait," in Anderson's usage, the artifact of Osmond's creation)—the complete collapse, in short, of Isabel's idealistic flight as it has projected itself into the marriage with Osmond. What the final portion of the book also gives, though few commentators on the novel seem to have taken note of it, is Isabel's growing mastery of the manipulation of appearances—her moving, in effect, into the territory of Madame Merle.[33]

It has been observed that Isabel, in the latter part of the book, is in the position to make Pansy's marriage to Warburton, just as Madame Merle has earlier been in the position to make Isabel's to Osmond. It has not been observed, I think, that Isabel's destruction, by means of a carefully placed word with both Warburton and Ralph, of Warburton's suit, even while she seems to further it, is as subtle a duplicity as Madame Merle's manipulation of her and that she to such an extent merits those charges which Osmond and Madame Merle lay upon her. (It is a further interesting complication that—although we approve of Isabel's action and disapprove of Madame Merle's, and although Madame Merle makes a marriage while Isabel prevents one—neither woman acts so much from self-interest as from the desire to benefit another, in both cases Pansy, though in each case the benefits intended to accrue to Pansy would serve to make up for the losses sustained by her benefactress.) Thus, as a study of the heroine's adopting the tactics of the opposition, *The Portrait of a Lady* definitely looks forward to *The Golden Bowl*, though Isabel's performance is neither so complex, thorough, nor successful as Maggie's.[34]

As for the novel's problematic ending, Dorothea Krook has provided a cogent answer to those who cannot fathom Isabel's return to Osmond, though her terms are not the ones employed by this study. Isabel must at the end, as Miss Krook suggests, accept the responsibility for her own actions. She must act as though she had been free, even though she has learned that her freedom had been drastically curtailed, that she had been manipulated by others.[35] At the same time Isabel has, I think, come to a radically altered sense of herself and her own freedom, one which recognizes the impossibility of infinite aspiration and realizes, along the lines she has suggested immediately prior to her marriage, that freedom can exist only within that finitude which results from the interaction of the self and everything external to it.[36] Isabel is in a sense freed from her desire for total freedom, but her new freedom must exist within the context which that desire has in large measure created for her. For if Isabel has despite herself been led and used, she has at the same time been so manipulated largely *because* of herself. Her own concept of herself has necessitated the choice which she has made, and her predicament has thus indeed been of her own doing. To this extent, at least, is her acceptance of the consequences which she sees herself as having freely brought about a valid one.

This understanding of Isabel in the final pages is not, I think, contradicted by the tensions in her mind as she travels away from Rome toward her cousin Ralph and turns her thoughts to the ultimate extension of her old passivity and withdrawal:

> She envied Ralph his dying, for if one were thinking of rest that was the most perfect of all. To cease utterly, to give it all up and not know anything more—this idea was as sweet as the vision of a cool bath in a marble tank, in a darkened chamber, in a hot land.
>
> She had moments indeed in her journey from Rome which were almost as good as being dead. She sat in her corner, so motionless, so passive, simply with the sense of being carried, so detached from hope and regret, that she recalled to herself one of those Etruscan figures couched upon the receptacle of their ashes. (NY, IV:391)

Not to know anything more—the death wish, which is the antithesis of her aspiration to know everything, becomes its fulfilment, just as her realm of ideality imaginatively fulfills itself in the cold stasis of the figure upon the urn, the portrait of a lady that is "dead, dead, dead." And half a page later the mode of aspiration returns in its indeterminacy:

> Deep in her soul—deeper than any appetite for renunciation —was the sense that life would be her business for a long time to come. And at moments there was something inspiring, almost enlivening, in the conviction. It was a proof of strength —it was a proof she should some day be happy again. It could n't be she was to live only to suffer; she was still young, after all, and a great many things might happen to her yet. To live only to suffer—only to feel the injury of life repeated and enlarged—it seemed to her she was too valuable, too capable, for that. Then she wondered if it were vain and stupid to think so well of herself. When had it ever been a guarantee to be valuable? Was n't all history full of the destruction of precious things? Was n't it much more probable that if one were fine one would suffer? It involved then perhaps an admission that one had a certain grossness; but Isabel recognized, as it passed before her eyes, the quick vague shadow of a long future. She should never escape; she should last to the end. Then the middle years wrapped her about again and the grey curtain of her indifference closed her in. (NY, IV:392–393)

It is the old mode, but with a difference, even if the hope that "things might happen to her yet" recalls her old, unconscious retreat to that passivity where one's moves are determined for one. This mode is less an inclusive and hence objectless aspiration than it is a resignation—an awareness, occasioned by suffering, of the self's conceivable grossness—to one's continuing to live and experience in a world the grossness of which is its finitude. And so this near-climactic meditation, internally contradictory as it is, sounds Isabel's gained awareness at the same time that it echoes those paradoxical flights and retreats which are her very continuity.

XIII

To trace the function of money in so organic and complex a novel as *The Portrait of a Lady* is, ultimately, to trace the history of those consciousnesses and the development of those themes with which it comes into contact and which it is meant to illuminate—indeed, our analysis serves little purpose unless it demonstrates the inextricability of this particular category of symbols from the work as a whole. Such inextricability is particularly the case in the revised version of the *Portrait*, where "commercial" images abound, particularly in the mind of Isabel, and clearly show the impossibility of assigning a fixed set of connotations or thematic overtones. It would be easy enough simply to align money with the "commercial" attitude shared to a degree by Osmond and Madame Merle (though their differences, and the higher degree of sophistication and complexity possessed by Madame Merle, should be thoroughly apparent)—the attitude of use, exploitation, reification, externality. Such a simplification would, however, eliminate from consideration Ralph's view of money in his bestowal of half his inheritance upon Isabel, as well as Isabel's own complex and vacillating sense.

There are, as we have seen, two polar sets of meaning associated with money in the novel—money as cash, as, to the idealistic consciousness, the limiting envelope of circumstances; and money as imaginative potential, the self-created symbol of the idealistic consciousness; and these two sets of meanings, abstracted from the *Portrait*, reinforce the polar categories set forth at the beginning of this study.

But the abstraction is not the whole picture, for *The Portrait of a Lady* is no mere confrontation of diametrically opposed poles. It is, rather, the history of consciousness entering into negotiation with the world external to it, and the meaning of the symbol fluctuates and changes as it participates in those negotiations. For money is not just "cash" and/or "imagination"; it symbolizes the entire realm of thought from which it can be seen as either. As a huge fortune, it is both the prodigious giver of freedom and the prodigious limiter. By extension, as Isabel's consciousness converts it into symbol, it becomes equivalent to free agency, to consciousness itself, and to the whole finite, external world of choice and action which limits freedom. As a fact, it is both brute and imaginative—and also somewhere in between, as the imagination apprehends its brutishness. It is a fact external to and independent of Isabel; it is a fact seen as such and hence as limiting by Isabel; it is a fact, because so perceived, dependent upon her; and finally it is a fact seen as internal and correlative with the self's wealth of potential.

Money symbolizes the ideal and the actual, the potential and the mutable; it is both the voice of the nightingale and the cry forlorn. But it is a symbol only as the novel's central character so treats it. Its dual symbolism results from Isabel's imaginatively viewing it as the surrogate both of herself and of that world which she seeks simultaneously to embrace and escape. And so *The Portrait of a Lady*, like *Moby-Dick*, like any novel concerning Idealism, one is tempted to say, is less a symbolic novel than a novel about the symbolic imagination—about the mind's coming to terms with itself and the world, imposing categories upon or discovering them in the welter of the world's detail, finding meaning in particularity and extending it to generality. And if, in the novel, money can be said to be symbolically anterior to Isabel's conscious apprehension of it, it is in the reader's beyond or before her submitting it to the same extension, viewing it as the token brute fact of the world ever impervious to consciousness's aggrandizement, the limiting but liberating condition of the external with which the choice not to interact is itself an interaction. The extension, the admission of externality, is in itself, however, a conversion—the will is battered upon the indifferent fact of the world, but in the statement's making the world has already become idea.

CHAPTER FIVE

The Golden Bowl

Der Mensch ist Herr der Gegensätze, sie sind durch ihn, und also ist er vornehmer als sie.

— Der Zauberberg

I

The Golden Bowl begins at that level of figurative complexity on which the revised *Portrait of a Lady* concluded, and the complexity is heightened by the large imperviousness of the heroine, Maggie Verver, to its existence. Whereas Isabel Archer moves from a philosophically ensured innocence to negotiation with the terms of an alien philosophy, Maggie Verver's innocence rests upon the foundation of what Isabel consciously abjured, and her progression is toward the consciousness of foundations and their implications for both damnation and salvation. The dual symbolism of money—as liberator and limit, as figure for both imaginative magnanimity and manipulative violation—is the paradoxical suspension toward which the *Portrait* works; but the suspension is itself the *donnée* of *The Golden Bowl*, the ambient medium wherein the Ververs move with an innocent ease which carries them out of the reach of paradox—the tranquil synthesis which must be subject to analysis, which must be consciously apprehended finally as paradox, before true synthesis can be achieved.

In *The Golden Bowl* there is none of the easy opposition of theories which characterizes *The Portrait of a Lady* at its outset, no diametrical juxtaposition of theories of the self. Though the attitude of the Prince and Charlotte is essentially opposed to the somewhat impenetrable one of Adam and Maggie, the novel's beginning abruptly makes clear that the two sets have a terminology in common and that the Ververs' sense unconsciously includes that of the worldlings—unconsciously because the Ververs at that point understand neither their *sposi* nor themselves. It is the unconsciousness and the ease which permit the initial fusion and create the initial difficulty, and which invite, at the same time, the betrayal that leads to knowledge and redefinition. To apprehend the redefinition, we must first examine the initial synthesis and its terms.

It is, the initial synthesis, the curious combination of the Ververs' much celebrated "moral sense," upon which the Prince discourses to Fanny Assingham in Chapter II (*GB*, I:32), and Adam Verver's prodigious fortune. For many critics, this combination goes beyond paradox to sheer incongruity, and the resultant misunderstanding has produced far too many one-sided readings of *The Golden Bowl*. Ferner Nuhn was one of the first to be troubled by James's treatment of Adam Verver. "James is at some pains to make Adam Verver seem consistent as a man both of great acquisitive and great benevolent powers," he says, adding that the novelist was unaware of the ambiguities of Verver's character. Nuhn postulates a reading of the novel—not intended, he claims, by James but unintentionally suggested by him—in which Adam and Maggie emerge as the villains of the book: "Power like Adam's, at any rate, that stands on a golden throne and holds a silken cord, cannot be granted for good without its being granted for evil."[1] This reading is probably far more in keeping with what James was doing than Nuhn admits to.

F. O. Matthiessen, for whom *The Golden Bowl* is the least satisfactory production of James's "Major Phase," balks at Adam's combination of fierce "acquisitive power" and "paradisal innocence"—neglecting the possibility that Adam's devotion to acquisition, until the famous transformation, has necessarily left him an innocent in other areas of life, has caused him in fact to seek relief in the innocent relation with his daughter

—and then goes on to observe that "Mr. Verver's moral tone is far more like that of a benevolent Swedenborgian than it is like that of either John D. Rockefeller or Jay Gould."[2]

For John Bayley, Adam Verver "remains a visionary figure, eloquent of the difference between the American millionaire as he was and as James would have liked him to be. So much the worse for the American millionaire, James might retort." But even so dedicated an admirer of *The Golden Bowl* is forced to admit that

> in the case of Verver this appeal to the artist's freedom in creation will perhaps not quite do. For one thing American millionaire collectors *did* very much exist, men who indeed saw "acquisition of one sort as a perfect preliminary to acquisition of another," but upon whom the metaphor bestowed on Verver's career—"the years of darkness had been needed to render possible the years of light"—would be grotesquely lost. So we may feel that Verver should be the Aristotelian "real because impossible" character, but succeeds only in being an unreal because improbable one. And it is this lack of coherence between Verver as a visionary figure and as a convincing personality that makes him strike us as a monster.[3]

The Jamesian rejoinder invoked by Bayley refers to the "supersubtle fry" in the artist stories of the 1890s, and one might simply refute Bayley's discrimination by pointing out that British authors existed every bit as much as American millionaires.

But waiving the criterion of verisimilitude, which Bayley surprisingly seems to trick himself into using, will not necessarily dispose of the criticisms of F. R. Leavis, for whom the Ververs are distasteful and acquisitive and the Prince and Charlotte at least palpitatingly on the side of life. For Leavis, as for Nuhn, the failure of imagination is James's, since, though he can be fairly explicit about Maggie's and Adam's acquisitiveness, "our attitude toward the Ververs isn't meant to be ironical. . . . That in our feelings about the Ververs there would be any element of distaste Henry James, in spite of the passages quoted, seems to have had no inkling."[4] The "in spite of" is a pregnant concession, though of an irony which is not an either-or proposition, of which Leavis seems himself to have had no inkling.

The Ververs' acquisitiveness has been a *cause célèbre* since Leavis, though many of the defenders of James's artistic awareness have perpetrated distortions undreamed of in the author's fuller vision. Extreme among them are those of Joseph Firebaugh, for whom the absolutism of the Ververs—Adam's aesthetic and Maggie's moral—becomes a total tyranny over their respective mates, and Jean Kimball, for whom Charlotte is the innocent and maligned heroine of the book, a surrogate Isabel Archer–Milly Theale–Minny Temple and the victim of an Osmondian Adam Verver.[5] Miriam Allott, in a more moderate view, and one which bears resemblance to Nuhn's version of the novel's unintended implication, sees James's statement in regard to *The Ivory Tower* as suggesting an attitude which permeates all the later novels: " 'the black and merciless things behind the great possessions' are now nearly always James's concern." For her, "In the last analysis their [the Ververs'] 'power of purchase' and their great possessions are revealed as the agents of a general corruption."[6] The meaning of that terminal "power of purchase," between which and its initial version the whole novel's redefining force intervenes, and the extent of its corrupting agency await our later examination. Before that, Mr. Verver's money, his presumed acquisitiveness, and how they figure in the book's initial synthesis of terms will be the subjects of our inquiry.

II

The standard charge, enunciated by Leavis and Tony Tanner, among others, is that Adam and Maggie Verver regard Prince Amerigo and Charlotte Stant as "things,"[7] that they have, in common with what James calls the "business imagination," a tendency to regard other human beings as objects for aggrandizement and extensions of themselves rather than as autonomous individuals—a tendency we have seen reach its cruelest fruition in Gilbert Osmond—and that this cast of mind remains unaltered from the novel's beginning to its end. Some evidence for this Osmondizing of the Ververs is provided by the references in the novel to Charlotte's and the Prince's "representing" their two households in the great social world: "Mrs. Verver was definitely and by general acclamation in charge of the 'social relations' of the family, literally of those of the two households; as to her genius for representing which in the great world and in the grand style vivid evidence had more and more accumulated" (GB I:321; see also I:322 and II:23). There is, nevertheless, a significant distance from Osmond's anticipation of Isabel's representing him and "publishing his style" to Charlotte's and the Prince's all too willingly "representing" the uneager Ververs on the public stage and publishing certainly no style but their own.

More damning, and hardly neglected by the Ververs' critics, is the first chapter's presentation of the marriage transaction as a totally commercial affair:

> "You're at any rate a part of his collection," she had explained —"one of the things that can only be got over here. You're a rarity, an object of beauty, an object of price. You're not perhaps absolutely unique, but you're so curious and eminent that there are very few others like you—you belong to a class about which everything is known. You're what they call a *morceau de musée.*"
>
> "I see. I have the great sign of it," he had risked—"that I cost a lot of money."
>
> "I haven't the least idea," she had gravely answered, "what you cost"—and he had quite adored, for the moment, her way of saying it. He had felt even, for the moment, vulgar. But he had made the best of that. "Wouldn't you find out if it were a question of parting with me? My value would in that case be estimated."
>
> She had looked at him with her charming eyes, as if his value were well before her. "Yes, if you mean that I'd pay rather than lose you." (GB, I:12–13)

Several things require attention here. The first is the unlikelihood of James's, with sublime oblivion, placing this passage (and many other passages in the same chapter) virtually at the beginning of the novel without any regard for the obviously ambiguous light it casts on the Ververs. The second is that this is just the first chapter and that the characters do not remain static for the nearly eight hundred remaining pages.

The third, certainly more problematic and probably more important, is a matter of tone. It is a hasty reading indeed which makes of the first chapter's Maggie (one of the very few Maggies to whom we are exposed in Book First, and obviously a very important one) a hard little acquisitor for whom people have the manipulable status of objects. Such a Maggie would simply be laying brutally on the line for the Prince the conditions of her having taken possession of him, a tactic even Osmond—who would seem to provide a touchstone for how far acquisitors can go in displaying their hands—scrupulously avoids.[8] The primary inference we can draw from the initial conversation is that Maggie's remarks are not to be interpreted as seriously intended, that they are uttered with an extravagance and a nervous gaiety which the Prince reads as characteristically American but which the reader can view as more peculiar to this particular American girl, who sees herself, even at the presumed crest of her early felicity, as trembling for her life and who later insists, "Yes, I live in 'terror,' . . . I'm a small creeping thing" (GB, I:185).

That Maggie is simply talking around rather than about every subject he raises, the Prince soon sees:

> He had perceived on the spot that any serious discussion of veracity, of loyalty, or rather of the want of them, practically took her unprepared, as if it were quite new to her. He had noticed it before: it was the English, the American sign that duplicity, like "love," had to be joked about. It couldn't be "gone into." (GB, I:15)

The almost totally serious little American girl is incapable of speaking seriously about love. She cannot communicate directly to her strange Prince, who presents to her as great an object of wonder as she does to him, the extent of her fascination with and the depth of her feeling for him; and she soars for escape from their pressure in giddy bursts of pyrotechnic language—

soon to be emulated by the Prince in his conversation with
Fanny Assingham (*GB*, I:27–28)—which achieves its larger
application only circuitously through its intended irrelevance.

This is not to say that the financial does not function
squarely with the moral and the affectional in Maggie's language—the fusion is one we have postulated her as easily accepting, her father's bank account and the habit of its power
giving her the freedom of the language—but to insist that the
meant emphasis falls on the latter. Maggie's repudiation of
knowing in any detail what the Prince cost is ample repudiation
of her thinking in cash terms, just as his value, which seems to
hover before her, is hardly a financial one. And when the Prin-
cess-to-be refers to what she would pay rather than lose the
Prince—using the nearly cliché language of emotional payment
which will become large currency as the novel progresses—she
suggests, in both ironic unconscious prophecy and direct statement of emotional capacity and power, the agony she will later
undergo to preserve her marriage.

Maggie's avoidance of emotional particularities (not to
mention those of dollars and cents) is strikingly demonstrated
in a flight of fancy to which she has already treated the Prince:

> "Oh, I'm not afraid of history!" She had been sure of
> that. "Call it the bad part, if you like—yours certainly sticks
> out of you. What was it else," Maggie Verver had also said,
> "that made me originally think of you? It wasn't—as I should
> suppose you must have seen—what you call your unknown
> quantity, your particular self. It was the generations behind
> you, the follies and the crimes, the plunder and the waste—the
> wicked Pope, the monster most of all, whom so many of the
> volumes in your family library are all about. . . . Where, there-
> fore"—she had put it to him again—"without your archives,
> annals, infamies, would you have been?"
>
> He recalled what, to this, he had gravely returned. "I
> might have been in a somewhat better pecuniary situation."
> (*GB*, I:9–10)

Maggie's extravagance is to an extent, of course, a measure of
her American Romantic fascination with the glamour of

Amerigo's otherness—the innocent from the city without a history is naturally drawn to the darkness which looms behind the incarnation of history—but if we take her literally, we must view Maggie as the antithesis of Isabel Archer, as the woman who eschews the self for the envelope of circumstance.

The little exchange concerning Amerigo's selfhood, immediately prior to Maggie's historical dithyramb, however, happily reinforces our reading of her tone:

> "There's another part, very much smaller doubtless, which, such as it is, represents my single self, the unknown, unimportant—unimportant save to you—personal quantity. About this you've found out nothing."
>
> Luckily, my dear," the girl had bravely said; "for what then would become, please, of the promised occupation of my future?" (GB, I:9)

Amerigo's words, of course, darkly hint in part at his personal history with Charlotte Stant, of which Maggie is virtually ignorant, but Maggie interprets them as referring to his individual nature, which she lightly deems her future object of scrutiny but of which, at least as manifested in his personal charm and the powerful attraction he exerts upon her, she can be presumed to have had several pleasing glimpses. Maggie is indeed no Isabel. She has no fear of the envelope of circumstances, for she has grown up with an enormous one—even though she may find herself a rather dwarfish figure within it, just as Amerigo feels the incommensurability of himself with the history antecedent to him. But for Maggie systems are not invidious, nor do they cancel the consciousness which inhabit them. Her ordeal will follow upon her discovery that she has understood neither systems nor consciousnesses, and her task will be to create new meanings out of the given terms which have impinged upon one another.

III

Even more suggestive than the tone of Maggie's utterance, however, and more damaging to the case against her is Prince

Amerigo's mode of response to what she says. If it is Maggie who introduces the financial note into the conversation, it is the Prince who descends immediately to the crude level of cash, while his future wife remains aloft in the metaphorical realm where money refuses to manifest itself in the coarse actuality of particular figures and remains obstinately, symbolically behind as a medium of ease and a power of attainment. It is the Prince who answers Maggie's whimsical paean to his history with the monetary cost which it has entailed; and it is he who insists that his value is measurable only in terms of what it brings in the marriage market, a descent the vulgarity of which he sufficiently, if somewhat baffledly, recognizes in the face of Maggie's refusal to talk, or even to think, cash. The persistent refusal is of course a large part of Maggie's charm and mystification for the Prince, part of the looming, intriguing American whiteness which either stubbornly avoids acknowledging what are for him simple facts or else converts them into scarcely recognizable versions of their familiar selves.

For if the terms of the marriage are repugnant to certain critics of *The Golden Bowl*, it must be remembered that they are hardly so to the presumed object of purchase, and that it is in fact that object, the Prince himself, who is largely responsible for the reader's conceiving the marriage as a cash negotiation.[9] Indeed, if there is anything disquieting for Amerigo in the transaction, it is not the contract itself, not the fact of being literally purchased, but certain contractual implications, evidently quite unliteral, for the clarification of which he heads at the end of the chapter to the moral enlightenment available only in Fanny Assingham's temple of analysis. The Prince has married for money rather than for love (his thick meditations in the book's early portion can at least hardly be said to be crowded with tender thoughts of Maggie), and the fact suffices to relieve the Ververs in part of the onus of aggrandizement. And Maggie is realist enough, we assume, to be thankful for an envelope of circumstances to augment the attraction of her own (to her mind) slight self for the man she loves, to allow her to convert what feeling he has for her into the equal of her own for him.

But Maggie's ease with the financial antecedents to the fulfilment of her passion does not issue in the Prince's turning out to be a crude fortune-hunter in the sense that refined Gilbert Osmond is a crude fortune-hunter, for Amerigo is in his own way as full of the converting and redeeming instinct as is Maggie, though for him what is to be redeemed is precisely that extent of history behind him which has produced his soon-to-be-altered "pecuniary situation":

> What was this so important step he had just taken but the desire for some new history that should, so far as possible, contradict, and even if need be flatly dishonour, the old? If what had come to him wouldn't do he must *make* something different. He perfectly recognized—always in his humility—that the material for the making had to be Mr. Verver's millions. There was nothing else for him on earth to make it with; he had tried before—had had to look about and see the truth. (GB, I:17)

By creating, with the means of Adam Verver's wealth, a new history commensurate with his "personal quantity," the Prince will redeem that part of himself "made up of the history, the doings, the marriages, the crimes, the follies, the boundless *bêtises* of other people—especially of their infamous waste of money that might have come to me" (GB, I:9). The anticipated redemption will later flounder, in the treacherous calm which the marriage becomes, with his fluctuating desire to pay off the vast mortgages on his Italian properties (GB, I:167–168). In the meantime, it takes it vagueness from his own as to what the Ververs expect for their money.

Their expectations, or rather his uncertainty as to the nature of their expectations, constitute the problematic element in the mind of a man self-admittedly without an excuse for a troubled consciousness: "For what, for whom indeed but himself and the high advantages attached, was he about to marry an extraordinarily charming girl, whose 'prospects,' of the solid sort, were as guaranteed as her amiability? He wasn't to do it, assuredly, all for *her*" (*GB*, I:20). That he has not by any means done it all for her—that if he can see the Ververs as having purchased in him a valuable *objet*, he can as readily see himself as having expended considerable effort to achieve that status—is driven home on the novel's second page:

> He had been pursuing for six months as never in his life before, and what had actually unsteadied him, as we join him, was the sense of how he had been justified. Capture had crowned the pursuit—or success, as he would otherwise have put it, had rewarded virtue; whereby the consciousness of these things made him, for the hour, rather serious than gay." (*GB*, I:4)

His gravity can exist even in the face of the "inspired harmony" which his lawyers have reached with those of Mr. Verver, "Mr. Verver whose easy way with his millions had taxed to such small purpose, in the arrangements, the principle of reciprocity" (*GB*, I:5). The culminating phrase, which refers ostensibly to the absence of demand imposed by the negotiations on the Prince, points ahead to the debilitating ease of stasis and stagnation which Mr. Verver's financial power will provide him and which will burden his mind in that phase of his life immediately prior to his and Charlotte's committing themselves to the betraying action under the guise of protecting the Ververs, under the cover of the terms of that sensibility which now figures as such a mystery.

The Prince is no mean fortune-hunter—he is determined to prove the most amiable and accommodating of husbands and sons-in-law and to fulfill the terms of his bargain, should the terms prove discoverable: "If there was one thing in the world the young man, at this juncture, clearly intended, it was to be much more decent as a son-in-law than lots of fellows he could think of had shown themselves in that character" (*GB*, I:5). The desire to surpass in decency "lots of fellows" is not perhaps the utmost expression imaginable of devotion to an ideal of conduct, but it is at least a patent refusal on the

Prince's part to do what he so easily could and what his lineage gives him so great a precedent for doing.

Uncertainty as to what he is expected to do, when the principle of reciprocity is so little taxed, is the troubling under-current in the curious mixture of elements surrounding him; and the curiosity of the mixture—the very fusion which Maggie takes so for granted—is the cause of the obscurity of expecta-tions. Thus he reflects on a now forgotten remark of Maggie's in response to his complaint about the pecuniary situation in which his remarkable ancestry has landed him:

> He had kept no impression of the girl's rejoinder. It had but sweetened the waters in which he now floated, tinted them as by the action of some essence, poured from a gold-topped phial, for making one's bath aromatic. No one before him, never—not even the infamous Pope—had so sat up to his neck in such a bath. It showed, for that matter, how little one of his race could escape, after all, from history. What was it but history, and of *their* kind very much, to have the assurance of the enjoyment of more money than the palace-builder himself could have dreamed of? This was the element that bore him up and into which Maggie scattered, on occasion, her exquisite colouring drops. They were of the colour—of what on earth? of what but the extraordinary American good faith? They were of the colour of her innocence, and yet at the same time of her imagination, with which their relation, his and these people's, was all suffused. . . . [He had told her then,] "You Americans are almost incredibly romantic." (GB, I:10–11)

This famous passage expresses the synthesis of values which, to the Prince's mind, should make for his total comfort and which yet, in its alien version of the familiar, disturbs him; and it hints a succession of images which will be subject to elaborate development before the novel's conclusion. The Prince's position here is not so much the previously postulated rupture with his antecedents as the apotheosis of that historical condition, but an apotheosis all commingled with the foreign element of the American good faith—so different from his own

—which is paradoxically both innocence and imagination. The bath is the Prince's figure for the Ververs' money, and it is an ominous forerunner of that "bath of benevolence" (*GB*, II:45) which Maggie will see the Prince and Charlotte as having prepared for her to protect her from the knowledge of their collusion. The implication is that both baths—the latter, the planned deception which passes for charity; and the former the charity, nearly *caritas*, which unintentionally deceives—are destructive elements, that submission to them will antithetically engender the action which leads to fulfilment, and that the former bath entails the latter.

The "gold-topped phial" (does it have a gold stopper, or is it, like the bowl, topped with a layer of gold?) is the vessel which embodies the Ververs' romantic imagination, and as such it suggests the golden bowl in one of its aspects. ("The bowl as it was to have been" is the later hypothesized fulfilment of the romantic imagination, though with its terms redefined by the test of experience.) The shape of the "phial," however, is more suggestive of Fanny Assingham's "crystal flask" of analysis (*GB*, I:273), the antithesis of the crystal bowl of synthesis (the configuration of the originally flawed theses), but an antithesis necessary for the ultimate synthesis of "the bowl as it was to have been."

These are the reverberations which the Prince's trope will eventually occasion. What now strikes him is the extraordinary mixture; and what strikes the reader, in the light of the whole chapter and of Maggie's later bath image, is that the soothing effect of the aureate bath seems designed to lull the Prince into inactivity. It is the Ververs' accepting his inactivity, accepting his intrinsic worth without active demonstration, which puzzles the Prince.

What attitude the Prince takes toward intrinsic qualities is nicely pointed in an ambiguous conversation with Maggie regarding Adam Verver:

> "He seems to me simply the best man I've ever seen in my life."

"Well, my dear, why shouldn't he be?" the girl had gaily inquired.

. . . "Why, his 'form,' " he had returned, "might have made one doubt."

"Father's form?" She hadn't seen it. "It strikes me he hasn't got any." . . .

"Oh, . . . your father has his own. I've made that out. So don't doubt it. It's where it has brought him out—that's the point."

"It's his goodness that has brought him out," our young woman had, at this, objected.

"Ah, darling, goodness, I think, never brought anyone˙ out. Goodness, when it's real, precisely, rather keeps people *in*. . . . No, it's his way. It belongs to him."

But she had wondered still. "It's the American way. That's all."

"Exactly—it's all. It's all, I say! It fits him—so it must be good for something." (*GB*, I:7)

The Prince deftly makes the point which critics have been making ever since: that Mr. Verver can hardly have come out where he has—that is, with so remarkable a fortune—as the result of benevolence. His fortune is ample evidence of a "form" which seems at odds with his demonstrated goodness. Maggie, whose innocence of the money-making process may be presumed to surpass even James's, denies her father any form whatsoever, opting for that simplicity and formlessness in which the extrinsic is the effortless continuation of the intrinsic. But the Prince denies the efficacy of such moral worth—evident, as in Adam's case, though it may be—for maneuvering in the real world; and he shifts the ground of the discussion to the pragmatic, to the level of what a thing is "good for."

That the Ververs never raise the question of what the Prince is good for is both his comfort and his confusion:

He thought of these things—of his not being at all events futile, and of his absolute acceptance of the developments of the coming age—to redress the balance of his being so differently considered. The moments when he most winced were those at which he found himself believing that, really, futility would have been forgiven him. Even *with* it, in that absurd view, he would have been good enough. Such was the laxity, in the Ververs, of the romantic spirit. They didn't, indeed, poor dears, know what, in that line—the line of futility—the real thing meant. *He* did—having seen it, having tried it, having taken its measure. (*GB*, I:17–18)

The futility which Amerigo envisages recalls the consciousness of Merton Densher in Venice and looks forward to the very condition which the Ververs' consideration will have created for the Prince as his crisis looms, and he images both that possibility and his present confused sense in a striking passage at the close of the first chapter:

> He had stood still, at many a moment of the previous month, with the thought, freshly determined or renewed, of the general expectation—to define it roughly—of which he was the subject. What was singular was that it seemed not so much an expectation of anything in particular as a large, bland, blank assumption of merits almost beyond notation, of essential quality and value. It was as if he had been some old embossed coin, of a purity of gold no longer used, stamped with glorious arms, mediæval, wonderful, of which the "worth" in mere modern change, sovereigns and half-crowns, would be great enough, but as to which, since there were finer ways of using it, such taking to pieces was superfluous. That was the image for the security in which it was open to him to rest; he was to constitute a possession, yet was to escape being reduced to his component parts. What would this mean but that, practically, he was never to be tried or tested? What would it mean but that, if they didn't "change" him, they really wouldn't know— he wouldn't know himself—how many pounds, shillings and pence he had to give? These at any rate, for the present, were unanswerable questions; all that *was* before him was that he was invested with attributes. He was taken seriously. . . . It would come to asking [Mrs. Assingham] what they expected him to do. She would answer him probably: "Oh, you know, it's what we expect you to *be!*" on which he would have no resource but to deny his knowledge. . . . His own estimate he saw ways, at one time and another, of dealing with; but theirs, sooner or later, say what they might, would put him to the practical proof. As the practical proof, accordingly, would

naturally be proportionate to the cluster of his attributes, one arrived at a scale that he was not, honestly, the man to calculate. Who but a billionaire could say what was fair exchange for a billion? (GB, I:23–25)

Amerigo's meditation embraces a range of possibilities we have already noted. He is aware that the Ververs place upon him no demands for the manifestation of his value; that they eschew particularity in their dealings with him, as they do in all their mental traffic with life; and that as they have "invested" him with "attributes," they have postulated in him values which may very well be of their own creation and totally different from what he envisages his own merits to be. His value for them he figures as that of a possession, picking up Maggie's image of the *morceau de musée* but converting it into a form more in keeping with certain demonstrated aspects of his sensibility. He sees himself as presenting for the Ververs a rare, gold coin (the "purity" of which seems to refer to the aesthetic fact of his historical antecedents, rather than to their moral tone) — one which is indeed negotiable currency but which will never be converted into its "cash value"[10] by the Ververs, for whom its value is intrinsic, "essential," its "merits almost beyond notation;" that is, irrelevant to the particularity of market value ascertainable by the reduction to component parts. The image is his assurance that "he was never to be tried or tested," but it leads to the ambiguous proposition that, even though he is capable of estimating his own qualities, the fact of his not being so tested will render his actual value unknown, not only to the Ververs but even to himself.

The question of the Ververs' moral sense, which suffuses the entire transaction, comes down to the question of what they expect him "to do," but the entire thrust of his meditation has led to the answer that, rather than "to do," they expect him simply "to be"; they refuse to put him to test or trial. But "to be" for them, he realizes, may be even more of a test and trial than those he conceives himself as habitually able to negotiate, for it presents itself in terms unfathomable to him. "Who but a billionaire could say what was fair exchange for a billion?" and the question becomes doubly charged when the billionaire is Adam Verver.

IV

Laurence Holland, in his excellent essay on *The Golden Bowl*, has suggested Adam Verver's function in creating the linguistic medium of the novel:

> The drama of *The Golden Bowl* rests in large part on the tensions created by Adam Verver's money and the other values associated with the American character. Together they constitute a language which the others are induced to speak, and the drama's irony arises from the fact that the language of the new imperium does provide an effective medium of communication but threatens to rule out, by its very power and fluency, the "reciprocity" the Prince aspires to, the shared relationship he seeks, the veritable equality which communion in the new language might afford.[11]

That the Prince and Charlotte have a language in common with the Ververs we have already noted: it is the language of money, though the two "factions" mean by it very different things. By the end of the first chapter the Prince is already tentatively groping toward some apprehension of the Ververs' sense. And some of the tensions which Holland points out, tensions thoroughly prepared for in the first chapter, are later voiced by the Prince to Fanny Assingham in the typically Ververian terms which he has first tried out on her in Chapter II: "And, pray, am *I* not in Mr. Verver's boat too? Why, but for Mr. Verver's boat, I should have been by this time . . . away down, down, down" (*GB*, I:270). The tension behind these words, the result of the sheer lack of pressure applied, is rendered much more explicit in the Prince's meditations two chapters on; and the ironic fulfilment of his and Charlotte's linguistic adeptness will crown the scene which those meditations initiate when the *sposi* seal the pledge which is at the same time betrayal in the moral terms of the betrayed. Before we examine the novel's series of reversals, though, we must return to the linguistic source, to Adam Verver and his prior conditions which generate the "given" of the novel.

Adam Verver is James's first full-scale rendition of the American businessman since Christopher Newman of *The American*, and the difference between them measures the artistic distance which he has in the meantime travelled, even as his returning to a solid representation of the business imagination indicates a desire to reassess and redevelop the potentialities which he has seen inherent in it. In the two novels preceding *The Golden Bowl*—*The Ambassadors* and *The Wings of the Dove*—the acquisitive instinct hovers, in virtually antithetical ways, behind the action of the novel. In the former it is associated with the fortune earned in the manufacture of the famous unnamed object and with the *modus vivendi* which in the end Strether rejects and Chad purportedly will sell out to; in the latter it is linked to the unspecified action behind Milly Theale's fortune, from the specifics of which she averts her glance even more violently than does Maggie Verver, and which functions as a symbol and a means for her charity's power to rend and transfigure. In *The Golden Bowl*, on the other hand, the great acquisitor appears squarely at the center of the stage, if only for a few relatively brief scenes, after which he retreats to the wings to be felt as a controlling power rather than directly experienced. He is an acquisitor the likes of whom James had never theretofore attempted; and the subject of his acquisition, though prior to the action of the drama, comes in for a good deal of elaborate and involuted scrutiny.

Caroline Gordon asserts that it is "James's intention to present Mr. Verver not as a businessman but as a hero,"[12] though, as Oscar Cargill trenchantly counters, "why Verver cannot be *at once* businessman and national hero Miss Gordon does not make clear."[13] James's habitual mistrust of the business imagination *per se* might lead one to question this juxtaposition of the heroic and the acquisitive; but the juxtaposition does go as far back as *The American*, and *The Golden Bowl* does extend the terms of the juxtapositions James is willing to risk. If it is notable that James portrays neither businessman, Newman or Verver, in the role of businessman, at the occupation of making money—and this fact can certainly be accounted for by James's confessed innocence of the world of "downtown"—it is equally notable that he takes up Verver where he left Newman off, at the point of a thoroughgoing conversion.

Newman's first conversion we have earlier treated: the rather preposterous scene in the cab, in which the wealthy American renounces instantaneously the governing principle of financial acquisition and begins to grope his rather dense way through the novel's length toward the climactic conversion, whereby he will come to be at home with both himself and his money, if not with the alien world at large. In *The Golden Bowl* the density belongs to the prose instead of the hero. Adam Verver is thoroughly at home with the easy synthesis of himself, his money, and the world. The ease of acceptance, however, especially in the case of Maggie, argues a simplicity very different in kind from—but perhaps more dangerous than —Christopher Newman's brash assurance that the best of Europe is his for the asking. (Adam Verver, for one thing, is in a far better position than Newman to know what the best of Europe is. The aesthetic passion which burns so brightly in Verver remains dormant in Newman throughout *The American*.)

This simplicity is what so many critics have refused to swallow, and even Cargill, who is not the man to sell either Henry James or Adam Verver short, will not buy it: "Verver's simplicity does not accord with his business history and this fact alone should set us on guard against accepting the estimates of the Prince, Charlotte, the Assinghams, and even Maggie, on him. It would seem instead a guise behind which he could operate in enigmatic security." Again: "His 'innocence' is the manufacture of other characters in the novel and should be discounted."[14] Cargill is evidently with the Prince in seeing Adam Verver as possessing a definite "form," but his wholesale dismissal of Verver's "innocence" tends to drive *The Golden Bowl* into the solipsistic camp of *The Sacred Fount*.

The Golden Bowl does indeed call into question the reliability of the subjective, imaginative vision and hence the reliability of the other characters' appraisal of Adam Verver and even his self-appraisal—Maggie's being riven with doubt as to the integrity of her hypotheses in Book Second is a full, but not the only, demonstration of this major theme[15]—but it just as clearly progresses toward an expansion of consciousness, a growth of the individual vision to include the terms of others and to actualize its own. The shifting of appearance in *The Golden Bowl*, more than in almost any other novel, renders the definitiveness of any term problematic; but the significant terms achieve a reality of their own, and Adam's innocence becomes finally as meaningful as his craft and his power, becomes even continuous with them.

As he has presented in the first chapter of Part First the revelatory conversation and imagistic density necessary to an understanding of the Prince and Maggie, so in the first two chapters of Part Second, James provides the basis for an understanding of Adam Verver. It is in the thickness of Verver's rumination while Mrs. Rance hovers with her hand on the billiard-room door that the reader gains a view of the consciousness which has brought him out at the place the Prince has found him. Mr. Verver is himself aware of that innocence which is constantly being attributed to him, but he localizes it in the benighted past before his conversion—the benightedness of which has extended to the lack of that moral appraisal of his own activity which is now vouchsafed him:

> It was the strange scheme of things again: the years of darkness had been needed to render possible the years of light. A wiser hand than he at first knew had kept him hard at acquisition of one sort as a perfect preliminary to acquisition of another, and the preliminary would have been weak and wanting if the good faith of it had been less. His comparative blindness had made the good faith, which in its turn had made the soil propitious for the flower of the supreme idea. (*GB*, I:146)

It will be, of course, the strange scheme of things again before the novel is over: the period of darkness which is the false equilibrium is needed to render possible what final illumination exists. By "good faith" Verver obviously means his former belief in his acquisitive occupation and his inability to question its moral rectitude; and though the question, as his subsequent reflection will show, is now thoroughly open to him, his previous blindness shadows his present good faith and renders its ethical status ambiguous as well.

The dedication to sheer acquisition has been a delusion, an exclusion; his mind's propensity has all the time been for its opposite. But even the delusion has struck the idealistic note characteristic of the Ververs, and Adam's present description reveals the potentiality for conversion inherent in it:

> He had had to *like* forging and sweating, he had had to like polishing and piling up his arms. They were things at least he had had to believe he liked, just as he had believed he liked transcendent calculation and imaginative gambling all for themselves, the creation of "interests" that were the extinction of other interests, the livid vulgarity, even, of getting in, or getting out, first. That had of course been so far from really the case—with the supreme idea, all the while, growing and striking deep, under everything, in the warm, rich earth. . . . The fact itself, the fact of his fortune, would have been a barren fact enough if the first sharp tender shoot had never struggled into day. . . . He was happier, doubtless, than he deserved; but *that*, when one was happy at all, it was easy to be. He had wrought by devious ways, but he had reached the place, and what would ever have been straighter, in any man's life, than his way, now, of occupying it? (GB, I:146–147)

Recognition of the early deviousness is what critics seem unwilling to grant Adam Verver, not to mention the justice of his observation on happiness, or the possibility of a happiness untainted by the tone of the old deviousness. Such recognition is hardly justification of a new deviousness, unsensed by Verver; but the intervening conversion must be acknowledged, and critics loath to admit the power for conversion of the human imagination are better off not reading Henry James.

Adam's conversion from the business imagination is even

less concretized for the reader than Newman's, but it figures for
Adam as the rendering of poetic image into psychic fact:

> He had, like many other persons, in the course of his reading,
> been struck with Keats's sonnet about stout Cortez in the
> presence of the Pacific; but few persons, probably had so de-
> voutly fitted the poet's grand image to a fact of experience.
> It consorted so with Mr. Verver's consciousness of the way in
> which, at a given moment, he had stared at his Pacific, that a
> couple of perusals of the immortal lines had sufficed to stamp
> them in his memory. His "peak in Darien" was the sudden
> hour that had transformed his life, the hour of his perceiving
> with a mute inward gasp akin to the low moan of apprehensive
> passion, that a world was left him to conquer and that he might
> conquer it if he tried. It had been a turning of the page of
> the book of life—as if a leaf long inert had moved at a touch
> and, eagerly reversed, had made such a stir of the air as sent
> up into his face the very breath of the Golden Isles. To rifle
> the Golden Isles had, on the spot, become the business of his
> future, and with the sweetness of it—what was the most won-
> drous of all—still more even in the thought than in the act.
> (GB, I:142)

The priority of thought to action characterizes the converted
Adam Verver; and when he reflects, in connection with the
opening of the American City museum, that "his imagination
. . . got over the ground faster than his judgment" (GB, I:147),
we are reminded of Isabel Archer's early sense of her imagination, with its tendency to entertain contradictories, and of
Adam's own deluded "creation of 'interests' that were the extinction of other interests." That imaginative suspension is
recapitulated in Adam's later version of his conversion—a high
subtilization of Christopher Newman's, in which the conventional self had gaped at the doings of a newly emergent self.
Adam's epiphany, in contrast, is the gradual overcoming of the
dichotomy, as the conventional self grows at home in the mental domain of the other, the real self:

> His real friend, in all the business, was to have been his own
> mind, with which nobody had put him in relation. He had
> knocked at the door of that essentially private house, and his

call, in truth, had not been immediately answered; so that
when, after waiting and coming back, he had at last got in, it
was, twirling his hat, as an embarrassed stranger, or, trying his
keys, as a thief at night. He had gained confidence only with
time, but when he had taken real possession of the place it
had been never again to come away. (GB, I:151)

The reality with which the old Adam has come to terms
is the self moved by "the aesthetic principle" (GB, I:200),
the abstract acquisitive drive converted into acquisition of a
higher order—the relish of achieved perfection of surface, which
issues, by means of his earlier acquisition's fruits, in the grand
design for the American City museum. That design and the
presumed taste behind it—Adam's celebration of "the affinity of
Genius, or at least of Taste, with something in himself" (GB,
I:142)—have been thoroughly debunked by the anti-Jacobites
and anti-Ververites, particularly Maxwell Geismar, whose certainty about "life" and its possibilities is even more remarkable
than that of Leavis;[16] but even so subtle and satisfying a critic
of James as Frederick C. Crews has seen Adam as largely the
target of authorial irony:

> Not only are his collections, his relationship with Maggie, and
> his projects for the utopian American City all part of a na-
> tional obsession with the ideal, they all fall characteristically
> short of the real. . . . James is thus at his most ironical when
> speaking of Adam's perceptiveness. Adam thinks he is com-
> bining American simplicity with the taste of a connoisseur of
> art. . . . What he is really doing is admiring an image of him-
> self that he has drawn from his concept of perfection—i.e.
> from the marriage of power and taste. But if his power is real,
> we are led to believe that his taste is specious. "He cared that
> a work of art of price should 'look like' the master to whom
> it might perhaps be deceitfully attributed; but he had ceased
> on the whole to know any matter of the rest of life by its
> looks" [GB, I:149].[17]

The quotation which Crews introduces as evidence for James's
ironic treatment of Adam Verver seems certainly at first glance
to call the collector's taste into question. On second glance it

raises the question of whether a thoroughly convincing fake possesses less intrinsic merit than the actuality, and in so doing it suggests a more Jamesian approach to reality than Crews grants Adam Verver. Furthermore, Verver's having "ceased on the whole to know any matter of the rest of life by its looks" (and the fact of cessation indicates that the tendency was paradoxically part of Mr. Verver's former blindness) reveals him as a man who appreciates the beautiful appearance but whose knowledge of life does not rest, or does not desire to rest, on appearances. True, in Book First, Adam is largely unaware of the reality he has helped to create; his desire to penetrate to the essence does stop at the beauty of the surface. Yet in Book Second, given what he knows, Adam will act to insure that the reality coincides with the beauty of the surface.

Considering Adam's later pragmatism, as well as the contrast between the Prince's brand of pragmatism and the early Ververian idealism, it is surprising to discover what Crews isolates as the wellspring of Adam's error: "Lack of genuine contact with reality, then, is Adam's principal shortcoming. He is an expert on the relative usefulness of things, but he is incapable of discovering what things are. This condition, like his power, derives from his supremely American pragmatism. Indeed, his power and his weakness are two sides of the same coin, for a monotonous vagueness of mind is at the base of them both."[18] It might be urged that Adam's lack of contact with reality comes from accepting an idealistic notion of how things essentially are; that his apparent monotonous vagueness of mind is in large part the "iridescent cloud" which he generates —the appearance he creates for sheer affability of contact—and that the vagueness of pragmatism, which regards life as a malleable medium, is a different thing from the apparent nondifferentiation of Adam's monism in the novel's first half. That idealism and pragmatism have in common a theory of internal relation and an emphasis upon the reality which the human imagination can achieve increases the difficulty of assigning theoretical positions to the characters, but it also points to the possible immanence of pragmatism in idealism, and in so doing it suggests a reading of Adam Verver not wholly at variance with that of Crews.

Adam Verver's taste must be taken with some seriousness. For one thing, if the museum in American City were unambiguously ridiculous, then so would be the novel's resolution of Adam and Charlotte Verver. The possible absurdity is even deflected by James in the references to the ridicule heaped by American newspapers upon Adam Verver for his project. (The inclusion within the structure of the work of a reading damaging to his characters, in order to show precisely that such a reading is not the whole picture, is typical of James's late method. Charlotte's reference to Adam's and Maggie's "playing at 'Mr. Thompson' and 'Mrs. Fane'" [GB, I:254] both anticipates and nicely demolishes Ferner Nuhn's reading of the book's final chapter.[19])

Adam's vision, though it is marked by an ambiguity of which he is unaware and which it will be part of the novel's burden to render explicit, cannot, in the book's terms, be brushed aside lightly. In fact, its falling into abeyance while the grandfather-father plays surrogate father-husband is, as Holland indicates, one of the positive harms engendered by the debilitating stasis of the double marriage,[20] and its resumption to embrace Charlotte at the novel's end one of the positive values emerging from the subsequent redefinition.

The importance of Adam Verver's conversion is emphasized by Stephen L. Mooney: "The Keats sonnet, which Adam greatly admires, centers on the sublimation of the idea of conquest, translating the literal 'realm of gold' into a metaphor for states of intense consciousness. Like Keats' Cortez, Adam has had his own moment of revelation and has found in it the end of his question as to the meaning of wealth."[21] It is difficult, nevertheless, to go along with Mooney in finding Adam superior to the three other principal characters. One can agree that, as he says, "throughout *The Golden Bowl* it is Adam's consciousness that creates the possibilities of life for Maggie, the

Prince, and Charlotte"; but one must note that they are in part possibilities for suffering and destruction. Mooney also says that "Adam achieves moral omniscience by embracing art; the peace that passeth understanding, for him, is aesthetic contemplation. The Verver Museum signifies his church, with Adam himself as priest and provider." Even Adam does not go so far as to claim moral omniscience, and Mooney fails to demonstrate how embracing art might produce in him so desirable a condition. Mooney also fails to sense the troubling ambiguity in Verver's religion of art. The clincher is Mooney's notion that "by associating him with Keats, James gives Adam the right to be rich, for his wealth is of the spirit."[22] His wealth is just as thoroughly of the billfold, one might rejoin, bypassing the question of who has the right to be rich (Mrs. Newsome?).

Mooney has accepted the Jamesian usage of money as a metaphor for spiritual value, but he has forgotten that metaphor is a relation between tenor and vehicle which qualifies both terms and that The Golden Bowl never allows one to forget the literal meaning of the vehicle. Like Isabel Archer, Mooney accepts gold only in its converted, imaginative state; but gold thus converted, as we have noted, buys neither objets nor princes.[23]

Ferner Nuhn, for whom the ambiguity of The Golden Bowl was completely beyond the ken of Henry James, accepts as intended the impeccability of Adam's attitude:

> Now, how does naïve goodness approach this precious but deceptive thing [civilization]? It approaches it, of course, according to its own spiritual law, what Emerson would call the "law of man" as contrasted with the law of things. It assumes reciprocity of moral feeling, expects value returned for value, faith for faith.
>
> Much in this spirit Adam and Maggie Verver . . . come with their hopes and faith to the scene of beautiful civilization. They bring the best of motives, come holding out their largesse of fortune and good will, and expect a return, in the shape of "culture," equal to what they bring and extended in the same faithful spirit.[24]

Nuhn is quite correct in stating what the Ververs bring and how they expect to be paid in kind, and the irony lies not only in their innocent misapprehension of the Prince's and Charlotte's mode of currency but also in that couple's determination to behave in terms of the Ververs' "good faith," even using its language as the seal of their betrayal. But it is not so certain that the premises which the novel urges upon the reader are so simply Emersonian (or, we might say, so simply expressions of the ideas of the novelist's father) as Nuhn assumes them to be. Indeed, it is difficult to imagine that Henry James, after the fierce scrutiny to which he subjected Emersonianism in *The Portrait of a Lady*, would turn, in the fullness of his artistic maturity, to a bland "testament of acceptance," any more than did Melville.

It is not so certain, in short, whether Adam Verver's attitude is the "law of man" or the "law of things"—whether his converting imagination allows him to enter, even with the objects of the world, into that right relationship which (as Henry James, Sr., had it) ought to characterize human dealings; or whether his aestheticism reifies human beings and renders them pawns for his manipulation. The question then becomes that of whether the converting imagination can exist as such in the world of action or must preserve itself (as in the case of Milly Theale) through retreat and self-annihilation.

Adam's ambiguity and the suggestion that throughout the "law of man" which obtains for him is diffused a refinement of the "law of things" (and the converse suggestion that the "law of things" has been subtilized in him to a near-humanistic level) are most richly presented in a passage prior to the Brighton venture:

> Nothing perhaps might affect us as queerer . . . than this application of the same measure of value to such different pieces of property as old Persian carpets, say, and new human acquisitions; all the more indeed that the amiable man was not without an inkling, on his own side, that he was, as a taster of life, economically constructed. He put into his one little glass every-

thing he raised to his lips, and it was as if he had always carried in his pocket, like a tool of his trade, this receptacle, a
little glass cut with a fineness of which the art had long since
been lost, and kept in an old morocco case stamped in unef-
faceable gilt with the arms of a deposed dynasty. As it had
served him to satisfy himself, so to speak, both about Amerigo
and about the Bernadino Luini he had happened to come to
knowledge of at the time he was consenting to the announcement of his daughter's betrothal, so it served him at present
to satisfy himself about Charlotte Stant and an extraordinary
set of oriental tiles of which he had lately got wind. . . . It
was all, at bottom, in him, the aesthetic principle, planted
where it could burn with a cold, still flame; where it fed almost wholly on the material directly involved, on the idea
(followed by appropriation) of plastic beauty, of the thing visibly perfect in its kind; where, in short, in spite of the general
tendency of the "devouring element" to spread, the rest of
his spiritual furniture, modest, scattered, and tended with
unconscious care, escaped the consumption that in so many
cases proceeds from the undue keeping-up of profane altar-fires.
Adam Verver had in other words learnt the lesson of the
senses, to the end of his own little book, without having, for
a day, raised the smallest scandal in his economy at large; being
in this particular not unlike those fortunate bachelors, or other
gentlemen of pleasure, who so manage their entertainment of
compromising company that even the austerest housekeeper,
occupied and competent below-stairs, never feels obliged to
give warning. (GB, I:199–201)

Adam's monism is imaged here by a diminutive version of
the bowl. His littleness, which coexists with his greatness, and
never more powerfully than in the final garden interview with
Maggie, is stressed throughout the passage. The bowl this time,
surprisingly, is ungilt, though contained at least in a gilt-
stamped case; and just as the coin to which the Prince compares himself is "of a purity of gold no longer used," so Adam's
taste is "cut with a fineness of which the art had long since been
lost." But Adam's touchstone of taste differs from that of the
Prince, which at the end finds itself "all at sea" (GB, II:353)
in that Adam relishes "the thing visibly perfect in its kind,"

while the latter strives to be that thing itself. And if the Prince is ultimately presented with Maggie's idea of perfection, an idea perhaps unrealizable and certainly at odds with the merely visible—what answers that idea of Maggie's in Adam, what even prepares for it, will be seen to have been entailed, as Amerigo recognizes from the beginning, by a taste working in terms which go beyond the Prince's own.

Even more striking, perhaps, than the fact of Adam's monistic standard is that the narrator regards it as highly curious, curious preeminently in that the aesthetic principle has not corrupted Adam, as it implicitly might have been expected to do. The aesthetic principle burns in him, but with a flame cold and still—a flame the destructive tendencies of which are rendered inoperative by its paradoxically lacking the consuming heat and motion of process; a flame which feeds on a material no more combustible than "the idea (followed by appropriation) of plastic beauty." The parenthesis is puzzling: it seems to mean that the idea of plastic beauty is always followed by Adam's appropriating the object which represents it, but it could also mean that anticipation of appropriation itself serves as the fuel for the aesthetic flame. Despite this descent into the phenomenal, the near-Platonism of the passage is remarkable, and it confirms the dominantly imaginative satisfaction which we have seen Adam take in his collecting. The latter of the passage's two references to "economy" makes it clear that the economy referred to is a spiritual one, but the term itself just as clearly indicates the source of the spiritual condition. Finally, the reference to "spiritual furniture"—which looks forward to the much-debated treatment of Charlotte and Amerigo as "human furniture" in the final chapter—shows how inextricably the worlds of *objet* and spiritual principle are mixed in Adam's mind. The mixture is a successful one; but the final section of the passage, as Holland points out,[25] indicates how dubious a success it is, and the dubiety will emerge in sharper detail during the Brighton and Paris scenes with Charlotte.

James's making Adam's proposal to Charlotte rest upon the

purchase of the Damascene tiles has provided effective ammu-
nition for those who see the American millionaire as heartlessly
buying his wife, but the rich scene only renders actively explicit
what the passage concerning Adam's taste has shown, as it
crystallizes the impulses and ideas which have already moved
Adam and Charlotte to this point.

Adam's primary motivation in marrying Charlotte is, of
course, to relieve Maggie of the burden of feeling that her marriage has made her neglect her father; and it is one of the primary ironies of the novel's first half that his marriage will be
the condition for her unconsciously neglecting her husband, a
circumstance from which her stepmother will exact full profit.[26]
It has seemed cold and calculating to many—and the calculation, though not the coldness, can hardly be denied—for Adam
not only to marry for such a reason but also to present it as a
reason to his wife-to-be (GB, I:226–227). Adam apparently for-
gets in a later conversation with Maggie that making Maggie
feel him to be consoled was one of the reasons he advanced to
Charlotte for their marriage. There could be little reason for
lying to Maggie about it (GB, II:96–97)—but tell Charlotte
he does. Such a proposal indeed lacks the passion which some
find essential to the idea of marriage; but it has the virtue of
complete honesty about its terms, and Charlotte is certainly
both more aware than Amerigo of the terms on which she is
marrying (after all, she is an American too) and more willing
either to discount them (beyond her maintenance of a perfect
surface) or to turn them to advantage.

Nor is Adam's devotion to Maggie the only ground for his
proposal. "Well," he will tell his daughter, "I like to think how
thoroughly I was taken with her, and how right I was, and how
fortunate, to have that for my basis" (GB, II:96–97); and his
thinking is neither entirely after the fact nor entirely wishful.
His affection for Charlotte has been intensified by her having
introduced possibilities for higher human appreciation—even
if they are manifested largely in the comic relish of "type"—
into his heretofore essentially commercial transactions over

valuable objects, and his finding himself obliged to propose to Charlotte, after he has named in front of her the sum which he is willing to pay for the Damascene tiles, springs from the same impulse which moved him to allow her presence at the transaction in the first place. The complexity of the Brighton scene, in its familiar mingling of the commercial and the affectional, consummately reveals the fusions, tensions, and paradoxes which inform the novel to this point—the selflessness of Adam, which is a selfishness for his daughter; and the bargain for Charlotte, which is an opportunity for exquisite self-manifestation and exquisite duplicity.[27]

v

The Verver ethic, as we have noted, is founded on the principle of being right, on the submission of self-interest to consideration for others, though self-interest seems at first for both Adam and Maggie to be able to coexist perfectly with the interest of others, given sufficient good faith and sufficient abstract power of wealth to back it up. It is to be right to Adam, to remove the menace of Mrs. Rance and her kind, that Maggie brings Charlotte to Fawns; and it is to be right to Maggie that Adam marries Charlotte. Yet the terms of commerciality, which convert human beings into objects, lurk at the base of the Ververs' transactions, though an awareness of the fact that the rights of human beings, who are after all finite individuals, may not necessarily coincide—that one cannot inclusively satisfy the often conflicting interests of everyone—is restricted basically to Adam. Maggie, on the other hand, feels that the uses to which one puts people are recompensed by the benefits accruing to the victims of such charitable exploitation:

> "[Charlotte] hasn't a creature in the world really—that is nearly—belonging to her. Only acquaintances who, in all sorts of ways, make use of her, and distant relations who are so afraid she'll make use of *them* that they seldom let her look at them."

> Mr. Verver was struck—and as usual, to some purpose.

"If we get her here to improve us don't we too then make use of her?"

It pulled the Princess up, however, but an instant. "We're old, old friends—we do her good too. I should always, even at the worst—speaking for myself—admire her still more than I used her."

"I see. That always does good." (GB, I:184)

The worst does come, and that stage requires a delicate instrument indeed to determine whether Maggie more admires or uses Charlotte. The terms of usage, though, are totally familiar to the Charlotte Stant who accepts Adam Verver's proposal. She can, just as thoroughly as the Prince, approach her marriage in the spirit of a bargain, as she lets him know after the scene of their tremendous vow to protect the Ververs:

> "What could be more simple than one's going through with everything . . . when it's so plain a part of one's contract? I've got so much, by my marriage"—for she had never for a moment concealed from him how "much" she had felt it and was finding it—"that I should deserve no charity if I stinted my return. Not to do that, to give back on the contrary all one can, are just one's decency and one's honour and one's virtue. These things, henceforth, if you're interested to know, are my rule of life, the absolute little gods of my worship, the holy images set up on the wall. Oh yes, since I'm not a brute, . . . you shall see me as I am!" Which was therefore as he had seen her—dealing always, from month to month, from day to day and from one occasion to the other, with the duties of a remunerated office. (GB, I:323)

Or, as the Prince had already discerned for himself:

> What sufficed was that the whole thing, call it appetite or call it patience, the act of representation at large and the daily business of intercourse, fell in with Charlotte's tested facility and, not much less visibly, with her accommodating, her generous, view of her domestic use. She had come, frankly, into the connection, to do and to be what she could, "no questions asked." (GB, I:322)

But Charlotte is able to convert her sense of her use into doing what she likes, which is something radically different from what Mr. Verver expects of her. She has managed to convince herself of the absolute rectitude of her conduct by reviewing her offer to show Adam the Prince's telegram (GB, I:295), but the heroism of her act is considerably undercut by the fact that she has known her prospective husband well enough to realize that he would certainly refuse that offer. The mental gymnastics which allow her thus to deceive herself convince the reader, even the reader who sees the Ververs as instrumental in creating the predicament, of the essential speciousness of that straightness of appearance which she is fabricating. Her being used she converts, for Fanny Assingham's benefit, into the excuse (which it in part is) for being thrown together with the Prince, as if the forced yoking were altogether to her displeasure: "I'm, by no merit of my own, just fixed—fixed as fast as a pin stuck, up to its head, in a cushion. I'm placed—I can't imagine anyone more placed. There I am!" (GB, I:258). It will be the Prince's invoking Fanny's complicity in initiating the movement which has issued in Charlotte's present placement and his questioning, "Isn't it rather as if we had, Charlotte and I, for bringing us together, a benefactor in common?" that will bring to a peak Maggie's good friend's sense of the network of guilt and of the further possibility of duplicity (GB, I:272, 271).

Adam Verver has, with the advent of Charlotte to Fawns, sensed himself as participating in "a new and pleasant order, a flattered, passive state, that might become—why shouldn't it? —one of the comforts of the future" (GB, I:215). Of this passage C. B. Cox states: "The desire to be passive is always seen as retrogressive by James. Here it is representative of the Ververs' attempt to live perpetually in Arcadian bliss."[28] As we have seen in our study of the *Portrait*, the idealistic imagination entails an antithetical passivity, which in turn poses the danger of one's rendering oneself up to external control. The passivity which Adam Verver here seeks, however, is in a sense, a release from a life of activity. The importation of Charlotte has provided immediate release from the kind of acting, the "imitation of depravity" (GB, I:128), which was necessary to ward off the advances of various Mrs. Rances and Miss Lutches without the total breakdown of civility. The passivity which Adam now seeks is that which Charlotte's "representation" can supply, and its intended outcome is the harmony and equilibrium which the dual marriages are supposed to embody. But Adam, in achieving his passivity by bringing in Charlotte to act for him, has created a false equilibrium wherein the presumed "actress" can view herself as a passive creature acted upon and can use her presumed passivity and placement as a cover for acting according to her own design.

For it is their sheer fixity, their inability to do anything without Adam's and Maggie's pulling the strings, which becomes the note of Charlotte's and the Prince's consciousness during the latter portion of Book First,—the two are, by this time, as Fanny Assingham notes, virtually one—and it is almost for them as if their adultery were the sign of their good faith toward the Ververs. As Charlotte urges to the Prince: "Isn't the immense, the really quite matchless beauty of our position that we have to 'do' nothing in life at all?—nothing except the usual, necessary, everyday thing which consists in one's not being more of a fool than one can help. . . . There has been plenty of 'doing,' and there will doubtless be plenty still; but it's all theirs, every inch of it; it's all a matter of what they've done *to* us." That the Ververs have done something *for* them as well it does not at this point serve Charlotte's purpose to suggest, for it is her intention to convince the extremely restless Prince that the fruit of their proximity will be the inevitable outcome of the Ververs' controlling them as they do: "Nothing stranger surely had ever happened to a conscientious, a well-meaning, a perfectly passive pair: no more extraordinary decree had ever been launched against such victims than this of forcing them against their will into a relation of mutual close contact that they had done everything to avoid" (GB, I:293).

Colonel Assingham has, in the preceding chapter, cut through the metaphysics of the situation: "What in the world did you ever suppose was going to happen? The man's in a position in which he has nothing in life to do" (GB, I:281). And indeed the Prince is ripe for a disruption in the equilibrium so superbly "taken care of" by the still essentially mysterious Adam:

> Those people—and his free synthesis lumped together capitalists and bankers, retired men of business, illustrious collectors, American fathers-in-law, American fathers, little American daughters, little American wives— those people were of the same large lucky group, as one might say; . . . they hung together, they passed each other the word, they spoke each other's language, they did each other "turns." In this last connection it of course came up for our young man at a given moment that Maggie's relation with *him* was also, on the perceived basis, taken care of. (GB, I:297)

Though Amerigo senses that futility which will press him toward action at Matcham, he allows himself to remain passive so that his actions will be determined and so that Charlotte will bear the brunt of having chosen them, just as she will do all the arranging for the Gloucester expedition.

Earlier, on that rainy March afternoon when Charlotte makes her appearance at Portland Place, the Prince refuses to present himself for private conference should it emerge that his stepmother has come only to call on his wife:

> He should see, at any rate; and meanwhile, controlling himself, would do nothing. This thought of not interfering took on a sudden force for him; she would doubtless hear he was at home, but he would let her visit to him be all of her own choosing. And his view of a reason for leaving her free was the more remarkable that, though taking no step, he yet intensely hoped." (GB, I:300)

Taking no step but intensely hoping could well be a summation of Prince Amerigo, at least until he takes the step of sheer inaction, of not reporting to Charlotte the fact of Maggie's knowledge; and it is strange that this *galantuomo* even at the end seeks refuge in a frustrating passivity, that he is never really the equal of the far less gallant Merton Densher. If he will take

no direct steps himself, though, Charlotte is totally capable of
doing so; and the great scene concludes on the reality of their
passion, which both belies and fulfills their passivity:

> "It's sacred," he said at last.
> "It's sacred," she breathed back to him. They vowed it,
> gave it out and took it in, drawn, by their intensity, more
> closely together. Then of a sudden, through this tightened
> circle, as at the issue of a narrow strait into the sea beyond,
> everything broke up, broke down, gave way, melted and min-
> gled. Their lips sought their lips, their pressure their response
> and their response their pressure; with a violence that had
> sighed itself the next moment to the longest and deepest of
> stillnesses they passionately sealed their pledge. (GB, I:316–
> 317)

It is, amazingly, one of the most erotic scenes in English, and
it is the ironic consummation of the form of their good faith.
With it all form breaks down, gives way; all values melt and
mingle. It will be Maggie's burden to perceive the chaos behind
the apparent form and to shape out of that tangle of values, if
not "the bowl as it was to have been," at least a tenable
equilibrium.

VI

Discussing "The Path of Duty," Marius Bewley (who
scrutinizes the later James with a somewhat tenderer eye than
his mentor) speaks of a Jamesian tendency which culminates
in *The Golden Bowl*, the "reversal of values for the purpose
of revealing a deeper truth"; and in a discussion of Maggie's
terrace encounter with Charlotte he notes "an inversion of
ordinary human values, and even of appearance and reality itself."[29] But Bewley's reading faults James for going too far in
such a direction, and he takes a little too much for granted just
what ordinary human values are, as well as what is real as
opposed to what is apparent. Certainly our reading of Book
First indicates how subtly interactive are appearance and reality,
how thoroughly one system of values is implicated in an appar-

ently antithetical one. Given the tenuous syntheses of Book First, it is scarcely surprising that the basis for Book Second is one colossal inversion of values moving antithetically toward a new synthesis, an inversion which begins with Maggie's first glimmerings of knowledge.

John Bayley's fascinating reading of· *The Golden Bowl* is curiously marred by his seeing Maggie and her father's love as one which transcends knowing its object, as opposed to the love of Charlotte and the Prince, which seeks as its end knowledge of the beloved object (though his view that the Prince and Charlotte's "love is based on the successful carrying off of the tricky mutual pact which circumstances—in their view—have conspired to expect of them" is very suggestive indeed), and by his stressing the novel's obsession with "the power that may be exercised by *not knowing*, by the refusal to perform acts of visibly analytic consciousness."[30] The absolutist thrust, the transcendental urge of Maggie's ultimate passion does, it is true, move beyond mere knowledge (for one thing, Amerigo as an object of knowledge is rather disappointing); but the means of her fulfilment depend totally on acts of analytic consciousness.

Maggie's consciousness, in fact, once it gets going, is as fiercely inductive and analytic as any in James—it has to be to keep ahead of Charlotte's—and we can infer from Maggie's own inferences that the same is true of Adam. Maggie and Adam have, as Randall Stewart says, "learned to play the game";[31] but the game, the deadly earnest aesthetic play, is to gain knowledge for ends beyond knowledge, while concealing totally the fact of consciousness. The power which Bayley attributes to the Ververs is a result of the fact that their analytic consciousness is not visible, and it is their policy of concealment which Maggie learns from her husband and his mistress that begins the tremendous inversion of values.

For Christof Wegelin, "the shocking inversion of values is not of [Maggie's] doing. Her motive is to preserve her marriage, her means are determined by the web of deceit in which her life is caught."[32] Her motive, however, is more than that:

it is to achieve the reality for which the false equilibrium stands, to maintain simultaneously her integrity of relation with her father and her husband. Her father's marriage has ironically occasioned an unnatural closeness between herself and him which has allowed Amerigo and Charlotte to enter into a relationship which excludes them. Maggie's task, therefore, is to maintain the appearance, the semblance of equilibrium until she can actualize it. Significantly, after Fanny has shattered the bowl, Maggie can manage to hold only two pieces of her fragmented vision at a time. "The bowl as it was to have been," or whatever replica of such an artifact of the imagination can exist, cannot come into being until Maggie has accounted for all four who comprise her vision, until the wide symbolic range of the original flaw is recognized, and until Maggie's imagination has expanded to embrace those of her partners as the raw material from which a new reality must be built.

Whether or not the Ververs ever achieve knowledge of their own culpability has been hotly contested; but those muted, elliptical conversations between Adam and Maggie in Book Second point toward a recognition of guilt, coexisting with an attempt by each to conceal from the other the wounding fact of knowledge. Oscar Cargill sees Adam in the Regent's Park interview as offering Maggie a veiled corrective for her attitude and as insisting "that duty . . . to husband and to wife has primacy over affection for daughter and father." That Adam is more thoroughly aware than Maggie of the ambiguity of their position accords with our own reading of Book First, though Cargill's argument is injured by his holding that Maggie is mistaken in thinking that Adam married primarily for her and that he is attempting to deny the validity of her impression.[33] Insofar as Adam is denying to Maggie her importance as a motive in his marrying, he is trying to shoulder the responsibility himself for what has become of the marriages. He is trying, in short, to relieve her from feeling that, in being the cause of her father's marriage, she has also been the unwitting cause of his betrayal.

But Adam's language during the Regent's Park scene does also serve as a critique upon the perilous equilibrium which has permitted the betrayal, even though neither he nor Maggie will literally acknowledge to the other that any imbalance has occurred. The equilibrium now figures as the "charm" of their life—the term Maggie has introduced to signify that condition in her father which any voicing of her suspicion would forcibly rupture:

> She felt herself . . . her father's playmate and partner; and what it constantly came back to, in her mind, was that for her to ask a question, to raise a doubt, to reflect in any degree on the play of the others, would be to break the charm. . . . To say anything at all would be, in fine, to have to say why she was jealous; and she could, in her private hours, but stare long, with suffused eyes, at that impossibility. (GB, II:35–36)

And later it is so as not to "break the charm" that Maggie sees Adam as acting when he decides against their taking a vacation together—the ostensible charm being simply the happiness of their life as it is, but the possibly hinted breach being the further throwing together of their *sposi* (GB, II:55).

But Adam's discourse on the "charm" to Maggie is the fullest exposition of the paradox of their position, revealing as it does the selfishness inherent in selflessness and the immorality within morality, transferring to the shoulders of Adam and Maggie the burden of the charges which might well be levied against the Prince and Charlotte—and all behind the façade of their presumed perfect felicity:

> "There seems a kind of charm, doesn't there? on our life— and quite as if, just lately, it had got itself somehow renewed, had waked up refreshed. A kind of wicked selfish prosperity perhaps, as if we had grabbed everything, fixed everything, . . . It has made us perhaps lazy, a wee bit languid—lying like gods together, all careless of mankind.". . .
>
> "Well, I mean too," he had gone on, "that we haven't, no doubt, enough, the sense of difficulty."
>
> "Enough? Enough for what?"
>
> "Enough not to be selfish."

"I don't think you are selfish," she had returned—and had managed not to wail it.

"I don't say that it's me particularly—or that it's you or Charlotte or Amerigo. But we're selfish together—we move as a selfish mass. You see we want always the same thing," he had gone on—"and that holds us, that binds us, together. We want each other," he had further explained; "only wanting it, each time, for each other. That's what I call the happy spell; but it's also, a little, possibly, the immorality."

"The immorality?" she had pleasantly echoed.

"Well, we're tremendously moral for ourselves—that is for each other; and I won't pretend that I know exactly at whose particular personal expense you and I, for instance, are happy. What it comes to, I daresay, is that there's something haunting—as if it were a bit uncanny—in such a consciousness of our general comfort and privilege. Unless indeed," he had rambled on, "it's only I to whom fantastically, it says so much." (GB, II:94–95)

To Maggie it says fully as much as it does to Adam; but his refusing to name the particular immorality of Charlotte and the Prince, the suspicion of which overwhelms Maggie's consciousness, and his lumping the interests of the four of them squarely together represent a major surfacing of the terms of their imagination—a recognition that a beneficent prosperity is selfish insofar as it has "fixed" the Prince and Charlotte. And if Adam recognizes the consequence of his having had his wife and his son-in-law "in his boat," he senses too that he can steer the four to inhabitable land by maintaining the pretense that the boat has never rocked.

To Maggie as well comes the revelation that what she and her father have expected exceeds what can reasonably be asked —that Adam has expected his selfless selfishness for Maggie to be matched equally by Charlotte. Maggie's conversation with Fanny before the shattering of the bowl precipitates the girl's understanding of the possible extent of culpability. Maggie has urged that Charlotte would not have accepted Adam's proposal without both Adam's and the Prince's having convinced her of the feasibility of the marriage, to which Fanny replies:

"Yet Amerigo's good faith . . . was perfect. And there was nothing, all the more," she added, "against your father's."

The remark, however, kept Maggie for a moment still. "Nothing perhaps but his knowing that she knew."

" 'Knew'——?"

"That he was doing it, so much, for me. . . ."

" . . . The point is," Fanny declared, "that, whatever his knowledge, it made, all the way it went, for his good faith."

Maggie continued to gaze. . . . "Isn't the point, very considerably, that his good faith must have been his faith in her taking almost as much interest in me as he himself took?"

Fanny Assingham thought. "He recognized, he adopted, your long friendship. But he founded on it no selfishness."

"No," said Maggie with still deeper consideration: "he counted her selfishness out almost as he counted his own."

"So you may say."

"Very well," Maggie went on; "if he had none of his own, he invited her, may have expected her, on her side, to have as little. And she may only since have found that out." (GB, II:180–181)

Maggie is subjecting the terms of her original vision to criticism and analysis. She is beginning to see how innocence and good faith involve and entail their opposites.

VII

And it is in terms of their opposites that Maggie must act in Book Second—the terms of the world of experience and deceit, the actualization of an implicit tendency of her original innocence. To "act" at all is, in Maggie's terms, to abide by the false terms of that code of values which has deceived her, for to act is to perform, to put on a false appearance, and Maggie's position is rendered immeasurably more difficult in that her act is to appear not to act at all. It is the image of the actress which dominates her presentation in Book Second, since to take action at all involves one with the realm of appearances, and the first of a notable succession of figures occurs in Maggie's thoughts as she speaks to her father the morning after the Gloucester expedition:

> She reminded herself of an actress who had been studying a part and rehearsing it, but who suddenly, on the stage, before the footlights, had begun to improvise, to speak lines not in the text. It was this very sense of the stage and the footlights that kept her up, made her rise higher: just as it was the sense of action that logically involved some platform—action quite positively for the first time in her life, or, counting in the previous afternoon, for the second. (GB, II:34)

Action for Maggie implies "acting"; and it is her ability to abide by the terms of the opposition, terms all innocently latent within her own, that enables her to achieve her provisional success. She is now cast in a role similar to Charlotte's, and she even goes so far as to usurp her own peculiar version of the imagery reserved for Charlotte, being described at one point as a "timid tigress" (GB, II:10). In short, she must lie as the Prince and Charlotte have lied—her ultimate truth must of necessity be built on a false position.

In the two great showdown scenes with her stepmother, which further demonstrate the reversal of roles between the two, Maggie, in letting Charlotte "use" her, actually uses Charlotte for her own vision's realization. Charlotte is allowed to triumph in the world's—and her own—terms, but the greater triumph is reserved for Maggie's abnegation. If Milly Theale attempts to make the world ascend to her, Maggie to a large degree succeeds in forcing the world to conform to her terms by using its own.

The terms are thoroughly mixed in Book Second, as Maggie's consciousness extends to embrace antitheses for the attainment of a love which refuses to exclude. In her conversation with Mrs. Assingham, she asserts the frightening power which her feigned ignorance exerts and then asserts in the face of it her abjectness and passivity before what is imposed on her:

> "And that's how I make them do what I like!"
>   It had an effect on Mrs. Assingham, who rose with the deliberation that, from point to point, marked the widening of her grasp. "My dear child, you're amazing."
>   "Amazing——?"

"You're terrible."

Maggie thoughtfully shook her head. "No; I'm not terrible, and you don't think me so. I do strike you as surprising, no doubt—but surprisingly mild. Because—don't you see?—I am mild. I can bear anything."

"Oh, 'bear'!" Mrs. Assingham fluted.

"For love," said the Princess.

Fanny hesitated. "Of your father?"

"For love," Maggie repeated.

It kept her friend watching. "Of your husband?"

"For love," Maggie said again. (GB, II:120)

The inclusive love toward which Maggie works relinquishes neither father nor husband, and its extent is measured by the explicit rendering of the paradoxical terms which the meeting of imagination and world necessitates—the submissive passiveness which works people, the mildness which is terrible.

This expansion of consciousness to embrace logical incompatibles reaches its fullness as Maggie is able to empathize with a Charlotte floundering in her ignorance of the forces at play:

> The disguised solemnity, the prolonged futility of her search [for some respite from anxiety] might have been grotesque to a more ironic eye; but Maggie's provision of irony, which we have taken for naturally small, had never been so scant as now, and there were moments while she watched with her, thus unseen, when the mere effect of being near her was to feel her own heart in her throat, was to be almost moved to saying to her: "Hold on tight, my poor dear—without *too much* terror —and it will all come out somehow." (GB, II:292–293)

Maggie's provision of irony has been at least sufficient to sense the disparity between herself and the role she has been driven to play—most delightfully when she sees her having invited the Matcham party to Portland Place for dinner "as if she had sneezed ten times or had suddenly burst into a comic song" (GB, II:53). Yet she loses all sense of irony, all realization of the juxtaposition of incompatibles as such, when she is able to feel complete sympathy for Charlotte at the same time that she recognizes the extent of Charlotte's baseness. Maggie can find in

Charlotte the equivalent of what she herself has gone through, with the difference that Charlotte is incapable of grasping what Maggie has suffered.

Nor does imaginative grasp extend only to the inclusion of the antithetical but strangely very similar Charlotte—it accounts as well for the situation of the Prince and Adam. The scene at the end of Chapter XXXVIII, in which the Prince prowls in his unsettled condition through Portland Place, exists entirely in Maggie's mind; but in the light of what we subsequently see of Amerigo, it is verified as a fact of the mental drama of husband and wife. Similarly, though Maggie and Adam never exchange one literal word about the strait through which they are passing, it is through Maggie's mind—that is, through her certainty of Adam's mind—that his action in the final portion of the novel is accounted for. Their tortured, mute intercourse thus becomes the full imaginative rendering of a suffering and an exultation which involve all four together:

> "Poor thing, poor thing"—it reached straight—"*isn't* she, for one's credit, on the swagger?" After which, as, held thus together they had still another strained minute, the shame, the pity, the better knowledge, the smothered protest, the divined anguish even, so overcame him that, blushing to his eyes, he turned short away. (GB, II:301)

It is impossible to assign these responses to individual members of the quartet, for, as Holland says, these are the things "they all feel and know."[34] It is a community of anguish and potential triumph, but a community from which Charlotte's failure of imagination excludes her.

The cruelty of Charlotte's predicament has been seen as the crowning touch in the case for the Ververs' villainy; and surely James—or should we say Maggie?—takes great pain to insure that we shall not miss the extent of Mrs. Verver's suffering. For it is Maggie, after all, who is the measure of Charlotte's pain, as in the image of the invisible leash with which she figures Adam's power to control Charlotte. F. O. Mathiessen's comment that "James' neglect of the cruelty in such a cord, silken though it be, is nothing short of obscene,"[35] certainly goes far astray. Maggie totally realizes the cruelty of the figure, for the figure is of her own making. The cruelty is now inevitable: though the imaginative dimension of the scene is paradoxically rich, the possibilities for outcome in action are unambiguous. The only other alternative for Maggie and Adam is renunciation—and renunciation can at this stage mean only to turn over to Charlotte a fortune and a Prince for whom she is little more than a cipher.

The directness of action entails what seems to be the sacrifice of Adam, and Maggie's vision of a love which loses neither husband nor father would seem to perish in the act. But after Fanny has smashed the bowl, Maggie realizes that "she, for ever so long now, . . . had been living with eternity; with which she would continue to live" (*GB*, II:191), and it is *sub specie aeternitatis* that Maggie's communion with her father, horribly deprived of personal contact, will continue to exist. It is, in fact, that tacit imaginative communion which the latter stages of *The Golden Bowl* have celebrated, and its climax is the simple and profound testimony of belief which Maggie and Adam exchange at the end of their garden scene.

> "I believe in you more than any one."
> "Than any one at all?"
> She hesitated, for all it might mean; but there was — oh a thousand times! — no doubt of it. "Than any one at all." She kept nothing of it back now, met his eyes over it, let him have the whole of it; after which she went on: "And that's the way, I think, you believe in me."
> He looked at her a minute longer, but his tone at last was right. "About the way — yes."
> "Well then — ?" She spoke as for the end and for other matters — for anything, everything, else there might be. They would never return to it.
> "Well then — !" His hands came out, and while her own took them he drew her to his breast and held her. He held her hard and kept her long, and she let herself go; but it was an embrace that, august and almost stern, produced, for

all its intimacy, no revulsion and broke into no inconsequence of tears. (GB, II:282–283)

VIII

It is, too, this communion, which informs the final scene, when the inexpressible pain of separation brings Maggie and Adam to those highly relevant irrelevancies which fuse all the strains of the drama. The ultimate objectification of Amerigo and Charlotte has convinced many that the Ververs remain to the end the heartless acquisitors as which they presumably began, but the ambiguity which has attended the development of the novel's terminology should warn against such hasty conclusions:

> Mrs. Verver and the Prince fairly "placed" themselves, however unwittingly, as high expressions of the kind of human furniture required, esthetically, by such a scene. The fusion of their presence with the decorative elements, their contribution to the triumph of selection, was complete and admirable; though, to a lingering view, a view more penetrating than the occasion really demanded, they also might have figured as concrete attestations of a rare power of purchase. (GB, II:368–369)

H. K. Girling has commented that "the shade of irony which might adhere to the phrase 'power of purchase' is not felt in the context. 'Power' refers rather to the discrimination of the purchaser than to his capacity of acquisition as reflected by his bank balance."[36] That irony is indeed felt, and that it is of the rich variety which contains not only the meaning which Girling accepts and the one he rejects but also the imaginative power and depth of suffering which have allowed the four to come out where they have, would seem the more justifiable reading.

And where the four have come out is with the ability to preserve the appearance of perfect calm and rectitude behind which all their suffering dwells. It has been with such control— with the assurance, as the Prince sees it, of being able to "mak[e] her life" (GB, II:357)—that Charlotte has entered the final scene, and it is decisively important that she and the Prince are no longer "placed" but "place themselves," all the testimony of the rest of the scene being to the effect that their contribution to the perfect appearance is far from unwitting. The shame is still there in Adam's "power of purchase," but it is a shame diffused by that aesthetic perfection which conceals it and which bodies forth the possibility of a human harmony—the limitations of which can include the abysses of suffering—tractable in the real world. It is all appearance—the dominant note of the final scene is the concealment by all four of what is closest to their hearts—but the appearance too is real.

At the end the Prince sees nothing but Maggie: she obliterates his view much as the Palladian church which he formerly figured for Adam altered the perspective of the comfortable village square of the Ververs' consciousness. For it is doubtful whether the Prince achieves the fullness of vision to which Maggie has aspired and which she has largely attained. He can see at the end the pragmatic possibilities open to Charlotte, but his sense of the torture she must be undergoing is nonexistent. "Why is she unhappy if she doesn't know . . . that you know?" he asks Maggie (GB, II:357); and as Bayley observes, "This seems breathtaking in its callous insensibility, until we reflect that the Prince is honestly giving words to his total incomprehension of Charlotte."[37] But the Prince's incomprehension of Charlotte in his obsession with Maggie is simply his falling totally short of Maggie's empathic imaginative inclusion, and his failure renders him virtually as "stupid" as he has found Charlotte in her inability to grasp Maggie's value (GB, II:356).

Dorothea Krook sees in Amerigo "the final supersession of the aesthetic by the moral,"[38] and this is true in so far as it means simply the supersession of Charlotte by Maggie. When the Prince's touchstone of taste is "all at sea," so is the Prince himself. Maggie fills his vision but eludes his understanding, as desperately as he may try to identify his vision with hers:

It kept him before her therefore, taking in—or trying to —what she so wonderfully gave. He tried, too clearly, to please her—to meet her in her own way; but with the result only that, close to her, her face kept before him, his hands holding her shoulders, his whole act enclosing her, he presently echoed: "See"? I see nothing but you." (GB, II:377)

And the implication is that his effort to take in what she gives fails, that he is unable to meet her in her own way, on her level of consciousness—the intensity of his attempt, the obsessive self-abnegation of his desire to please, only heightening the transfigured pain of the scene. Maggie is now the creature of wonder for him that he was for her at the beginning, and his inability to know is matched by just as profound a passion. The reversal is indeed complete, and it is Maggie's sudden knowledge of the Prince's dependence which tragically illuminates the final sentence: "And the truth of it had, with this force, after a moment, so strangely lighted his eyes that, as for pity and dread of them, she buried her own in his breast" (GB, II:377). It is the tragedy which informs James's divine comedy —the ultimate synthesis of antitheses which the imaginative vision achieves—and it is the cost exacted, in lieu of that payment which the Princess refuses from the Prince's hands, when life and vision coalesce.

CHAPTER SIX

The Ivory Tower

" 'No vestige of any dead body was to be seen upon the floating
fragments. Log of the Defiance states, that a breeze springing up
in the night, the wreck was seen no more.' "

— *Dombey and Son*

IN 1870 Henry James had surveyed the possible inspiration
which an artist might find in Newport, Rhode Island. "I can
almost imagine, indeed," the future great novelist had rumi-
nated in *Portraits of Places*, "a transient observer of the Newport spectacle dreaming momentarily of a great American novel,
in which the heroine might be infinitely realistic and yet
neither a schoolmistress nor an outcast." Newport might not
provide material for tragedy—"Even in their own kind, the
social elements are as yet too light and thin"—but its tone of
moneyed leisure provided at least an ambient medium for the
play of sentiment: "Here, the multiplied relations of men and
women, under the permanent pressure of luxury and idleness,
give [sentiment] a very fair chance." Unlike Saratoga, where
"you feel that idleness is occasional, empirical," and that "most
of the people you see are asking themselves, you imagine,
whether the game is worth the candle and work is not better
than such difficult play," Newport is singularly free of the commercial taint: "Nowhere else in this country—nowhere, of
course, within the range of our better civilization—does business seem so remote, so vague, and unreal. . . . If there be any
poetry in the ignorance of trade and turmoil and the hard proc-
esses of fortune, Newport may claim her share of it. She knows

—or at least appears to know—for the most part nothing but results" (AS, 484–486).

The Newport novel remained hypothetical until the final stage of James's career, and the Newport which it was to depict was in many respects light years away from the one he had described in 1870 and was to recall in *The American Scene* as having been composed of "a handful of mild, oh delightfully mild, cosmopolites, united by three common circumstances, that of their having for the most part more or less lived in Europe, that of their sacrificing openly to the ivory idol whose name is leisure, and that, not least, of a formed critical habit" (AS, 222). The references to the "ivory idol of leisure," which suggests the title and the presumably central symbol of James's novel, indicates the possibility that for the "restless analyst" of *The American Scene* the new Newport was immanent in the recollected old; but it was the disparity between what he remembered and what his American visit during 1904 and 1905 revealed as real that the analyst took most pains to point out.

That visit, according to many observers of the Jamesian scene, was responsible for a remarkable *volte-face* in James's attitude toward the fact of money and its acquisition—an awareness, supposedly not vouchsafed him until that time, of what he terms in the *Notes for The Ivory Tower* "the black and merciless things that are behind the great possessions" (ANS, 1005). *The Ivory Tower*, Yvor Winters feels, is the first of James's novels to acknowledge the evil implicit in American financial life: "This form of corruption had, of course, been thriving throughout James's career, and James had shown little suspicion of its existence."[1] The dubiety of the pre-1904 innocence which Winters claims for James is amply shown by the novelist's treatment of the businessman from "Guest's Confession" through *The Golden Bowl*, and the case of James's awareness of the evil which money and its pursuit can engender has been well made by critics.[2] Yet if James did not achieve on his American trip a radically new sense of money, he did discover—and on a far more sweeping scale than he had imagined—an actualization of its most sinister possibilities which undercut the fulfilment of its better ones. Such was his experience of what had become of Newport.

To agree with Marius Bewley that the Newport remembered by James in *The American Scene* "had been an anomaly, even in the past, and [that] by the time James wrote *The American Scene* he recognized that the Ogres of the Trusts and the 'new remorseless monopolies' had taken over"[3] would be to accept James's appraisal of New York as covering Newport as well; but there is little doubt that F. O. Matthiessen is correct in asserting that James "had been deeply impressed with the transformation of the Newport of his youth" and that "he had figured this . . . in the image of 'a little bare, white, open hand' suddenly crammed with gold."[4] The treatment which Newport had received from its inhabitants—a treatment intended "to fill it substantially . . . with gold, the gold that they have ended by heaping up there to an amount so oddly out of proportion to the scale of nature and of space" (*AS*, 211)—appeared to James ultimately as a "violation," though the violation may have been meant as an accolade:

> There remained always a sense . . . in which the superimpositions, the multiplied excrescences, were a tribute to the value of the place; where no such liberty was ever taken save exactly because . . . it was all so beautiful, so solitary, and so "sympathetic." And that indeed has been, thanks to the "pilers-on" of gold, the fortune, the history of its beauty: that it now bristles with the villas and palaces into which the cottages have all turned, and that these monuments of pecuniary power rise thick and close, precisely, in order that their occupants may constantly remark to each other . . . that it *is* beautiful, it *is* solitary and sympathetic. The thing has been done, it is impossible not to perceive, with the best faith in the world— though not altogether with the best light, which is always so different a matter. (*AS*, 212)

The infusion of the commercial spirit James sees as in part a failure of the imagination, and a failure coextensive with "the best faith in the world." That is, of course, the terrific American "good faith" exemplified by the Ververs in Book First of *The Golden Bowl* and largely accepted by them as commensurate with their money. What James found, then, in the Newport of his American visit was the concretion of terms already realized in the act of imaginative creation. What he found in the rest of that visit, as recorded in *The American Scene*, and how it bears upon what he did in *The Ivory Tower* must be touched upon before we take up that uncompleted and hence enigmatic novel.

The surface of *The American Scene* reflects the hard, gold glare of money. There is "gold dust in the air" as James approaches the Jersey shore in the opening portion of the book, and the imaginative possibilities which the vista awakens in him figure as "golden apples." Expensiveness is the note of this emblematic prelude, an expensiveness all of the surface, preclusive of any relation, expressive only of itself. "We are only instalments, symbols, stop-gaps," the houses on the shore admit to James; "expensive as we are, we have nothing to do with continuity, responsibility, transmission, and don't in the least care what becomes of us after we have served our present purpose" (*AS*, 8, 6, 11).

The new New York is the apotheosis of the commercial. Its very appearance is "an expression of things lately and currently *done* . . . on the basis of inordinate gain"; its very power manifests "the candour of its avidity" (*AS*, 73, 76). Paramount symbols of the despoiling financial drive, as Dietrichson suggests,[5] are the American skyscrapers James described.

> Crowned not only with no history, but with no credible possibility of time for history, and consecrated by no uses save the commercial at any cost, they are simply the most piercing notes in that concert of the expensively provisional into which your supreme sense of New York resolves itself . . . Sky-scrapers are the last word of economic ingenuity only till another word be written. This shall be possibly a word of still uglier meaning, but the vocabulary of thrift at any price shows boundless resources, and the consciousness of that truth, the consciousness of the finite, the menaced, the essentially *invented* state, twin-

kles ever, to my perception, in the thousand glassy eyes of these giants of the mere market. (AS, 77)

The skyscraper seems "to have risen by the breath of an interested passion that, restless beyond all passions, is for ever seeking more pliable forms," and the obliteration of Trinity Church by one such "vast money-making structure" epitomizes for James the way in which the money passion moves toward the annihilation of all historic forms. The "fatal 'tall' pecuniary enterprise" finally looms as the extinction of style and of possibility (AS, 77, 83, 140).

Nor is New York alone fatally susceptible. In Boston the Park Street Church is to be torn down and replaced by a "business block," and even the new Public Library is "committed to speak to one's inner perception still more of the power of the purse and of the higher turn for business than of the old intellectual, or even of the old moral, sensibility." Everywhere he looks James finds "the overwhelming preponderance . . . of the unmitigated 'business man' face, ranging through its various possibilities, its extraordinary actualities, of intensity" (AS, 240, 248–249, 64). The America to which James returned seemed one possessed by that business imagination which the novelist's own imagination had rejected.

Quentin Anderson has interestingly drawn an association between James's reaction to the American skyscrapers as recorded in *The American Scene* and Maggie Verver's attitude toward that pagoda with which (at the beginning of Book Second of *The Golden Bowl*) she figures for herself the puzzling relationship existing among the two couples;[6] and he might have continued that the object which gives its name to *The Ivory Tower* groups itself as well with Maggie's pagoda and James's "tall assertive forms." James's repugnance for the tall forms, on the evidence of the way he treats the pagoda image, seems to predate his experience of the American skyscrapers and to issue ultimately in the symbol of *The Ivory Tower*, which accrues accordingly overtones from *The Golden Bowl*

and *The American Scene*. The associations into which the symbol enters, then, suggest its opposition to "the bowl as it was to
have been" and indicate the breakdown in *The Ivory Tower*
of the provisional imaginative synthesis achieved by Maggie at
the end of *The Golden Bowl*.

That *The Ivory Tower* is in some sense antithetical to *The
Golden Bowl* seems borne out by the figure of Abel Gaw, who
is drawn simply as the extinction of all those possibilities, even
those contradictions, which Adam Verver attempted to realize:
as the tower stands to the ultimate bowl (or the skyscraper to
Trinity Church), so does Gaw to Adam. The distance between
the two is pointed by James's grim pronouncement in *The
American Scene* that "the business-man, in the United States,
may, with no matter what dim struggles, gropings, yearnings,
never hope to be anything *but* a business-man," and by his
assertion that the commercial man's vulgarity comes from his
lacking any context in terms of which he might refine himself,
from his having become in effect *the* universal (*AS*, 345, 427–
428). Such a businessman—unregenerable, unconvertible—is
precisely what James gives us in Abel Gaw, the man who lives
only to ascertain how much money Frank Betterman, the man
who once swindled him, will leave behind and who is killed
by the news that that financial enemy is recovering.

To his daughter, Rosanna, Gaw is "incapable of thought
save in sublimities of arithmetic"; and when she comes to
meditate on the meaning of his life, "then most, frankly, did
that meaning seem small; it was exactly as the contracted size
of his little huddled figure in the basket-chair" (*ANS*, 869,
868). The effect is the opposite of Maggie Verver's meditation
on her father's paradoxical combination of smallness and greatness; for in Abel Gaw there is no paradox, no greatness, no possibility of the expansion of consciousness—only the constriction
and isolation of an acquisitiveness incapable of being translated
into a higher mode:

> He was a person without an alternative, and if any had
> ever been open to him, at an odd hour or two, somewhere in

his inner dimness, he had long since closed the gate against it and now revolved in the hard-rimmed circle from which he had not a single issue. . . . He conformed in short to his necessity of absolute interest—interest, that is, in his own private facts, which were facts of numerical calculation altogether: how could it not be so when he had dispossessed himself, if there had ever been the slightest selection in the matter, of every faculty except the calculating? If he hadn't thought in figures how could he possibly have thought at all—and oh the intensity with which he was thinking at that hour! It was as if she literally watched him just then and there dry up in yet another degree to everything but his genius. His genius might at the same time have gathered in to a point of about the size of the end of a pin. (ANS, 868–869)

Gaw's genius is the final ironic reduction of Adam Verver's, the stripping away of all possible meanings, all directions of consciousness save one: "the question of what old Frank would have done with the fruits of his swindle, on the occasion of the rupture that had kept them apart in hate and vituperation for so many years, was one of the things that could hold him brooding, day by day and week by week, after the fashion of a philosopher tangled in some maze of metaphysics" (ANS, 870). As a calculation which admits only one interpretation, it is in fact the breakdown of finance and metaphysics—that tenuous synthesis at which *The Golden Bowl* begins.

The breakdown is most evident in Rosanna Gaw's attitude. Another Jamesian "heiress of all the ages," she is Maggie Verver with a difference—a "big plain quiet" girl, who has (according to James's *Notes* for the novel) "no more taste than an elephant" and who is "only *morally* elephantine, or whatever it is that is morally most massive and magnificent" (ANS, 870, 1010). She is vested with the world's money, but her moral gigantism cuts her off from its use and renders it despicable in her eyes. In *The Golden Bowl* it was the curious fusion in the Ververs of the American moral sense with American money that most baffled the Prince. In *The Ivory Tower* the initial premise is the American moral sense's rejection of American money—a rejection, in effect, of both patrimony and father —as Rosanna's remarks to Graham Fielder while her father lies dying testify:

> "He's just dying of twenty millions."
> "Twenty millions? . . . *That's* what you mean here when you talk of money?"
> "That's what we mean," said Rosanna, "when we talk of anything at all—for of what else but money *do* we ever talk? He's dying, at any rate, . . . of his having wished to have to do with it on that sort of scale. Having to do with it consists, you know, of the things you do *for* it—which are mostly very awful; and there are all kind of consequences that they eventually have. You pay by these consequences for what you have done, and my father has been for a long time paying. . . . The effect has been to dry up his life. . . There's nothing at last left for him to pay *with*." (ANS, 933)

In the *Notes* to the novel James has further filled out Rosanna's position. Even as a girl persuading Graham Fielder to remain in Europe rather than return to his uncle, Mr. Betterman, she "has already in germ, in her mind, those feelings about the dreadful American money-world of which she figures as the embodiment or expression in the eventual situation" (ANS, 1001). Yet the Rosanna who abhors and refuses to touch her own fortune is capable of talking the dying Betterman into bequeathing his money to Fielder. Her act is a restitution of that chance from which she cut him off in their European association and probably also an atonement for her having chosen for him at all, for having in effect used him as an extension of her will. Rosanna recapitulates Isabel Archer's gesture of transferring to Gilbert Osmond's shoulders a financial burden—except that in Rosanna's case, the funds bestowed are not her own, even if they function as an unconscious surrogate for what burdens her—and the futile gesture of purgation will be twice repeated before the novel leaves off.

Rosanna's rapprochement with Mr. Betterman has come about, according to the *Notes*, "in the light of more knowledge and of other things that have happened. In the light, for instance, of her now mature sense of what her father's career has been and of all that his great ferocious fortune, as she believes it to be, represents of rapacity, of financial cruelty, of consummate special ability etc." (ANS, 1002). But if Rosanna's ability to come to terms with Mr. Betterman springs in part from her acquired sense of her father's at least equal financial culpability, its larger source is the change in Mr. Betterman's nature, a change which to some degree alleviates the bleakness of the breakdown sketched in Gaw and Rosanna.

In *The American Scene*, as we have noted, James attributes the hopeless vulgarity and blankness of the businessman to his lack of any other standard whereby to define himself, thereby suggesting the possibility of redemption, or at least amelioration, of the type in a superior context. The problem of wealth thus becomes a problem of identity, of the money-passion's attempt to concretize itself in terms of forms of which it has no comprehension:

> This effect of certain of the manifestations of wealth in New York is, so far as I know, unique; nowhere else does pecuniary power so beat its wings in the void, and so look round it for the charity of some hint as to the possible awkwardness or possible grace of its motion, some sign of whether it be flying, for good taste, too high or too low. In the other American cities, on the one hand, the flights are as yet less numerous—though already promising no small diversion; and amid the older congregations of men, in the proportionately rich cities of Europe, on the other hand, good taste is present, for reference and comparison, in a hundred embodied and consecrated forms. (AS, 159)

The absence of an effective context for the conversion of the money passion and what it accrues into something finer—basically what James had bewailed many years before in his *Hawthorne*—is the brunt of the passage. Yet the implication that, given a standard of taste, conversion would be within the realm of possibility mitigates somewhat the pessimism of the other Jamesian pronouncement that the businessman can never be anything but himself.

The standard of taste and the context for conversion are noticeably absent from *The Ivory Tower*, yet we are presented with a Frank Betterman who has, at some indeterminate time, ceased being a single-minded, avaricious being and become the Adam Verver of Book First of *The Golden Bowl*. That the details of Mr. Betterman's conversion, unlike those of Adam's, are thoroughly suppressed signifies, possibly, James's failure to discover in the America of his visit a likely context for such a reversal, though his treatment of Philadelphia and Boston in *The American Scene* indicates possibilities not touched in *The Ivory Tower*; that he does indeed present a converted Betterman suggests that the darkest of James's utterances in *The American Scene* are neither definitive nor preclusive of possibilities which his imagination could still entertain.

The Ververian quality of Mr. Betterman's imagination is perfectly evidenced in his interview with the thoroughly Europeanized Graham Fielder, who seems as much at a loss as did Prince Amerigo when faced with the similar mysteries of Adam:

> "I'm prepared for anything, yes—in the way of a huge inheritance. . . . If I only understood what it is I can best do for you."
>
> "Do? The question isn't of your doing, but simply of your being."
>
> Gray cast about. "But don't they come to the same thing?"
>
> "Well, I guess that for you they'll have to." (ANS, 921)

What Mr. Betterman wants Gray to be is precisely what he already is—totally alienated from the context of grasping materialism against which Mr. Betterman in his own conversion has turned. James says in his *Notes* that Rosanna will have impressed upon Mr. Betterman that Gray "is about the only person, who could get at him in any way, who hasn't ever asked anything of him or tried to get something out of him. Not only this, but he and his mother, in the time, are the only ones who ever refused a proffered advantage" (ANS, 1002). And Rosanna herself explains Mr. Betterman to Gray thus: "He had seen you in the great fact about you . . . that you are more out of it all, out of the air he has breathed all his life and that in these last years has more and more sickened him, than anyone else in the least belonging to him, that he could possibly put his hands on" (ANS, 938).

For Fielder, "being" and "doing" do not quite come out, of course, as the same thing, at least as far as the money is concerned, and he leaves the doing entirely to Horton Vint, not even seeking to ascertain the exact amount of his inheritance. The implications of this transfer of what may not even be perceived as a burden are quite complex, for Mr. Betterman has, in bestowing the inheritance upon Gray, reenacted the bequest which Ralph Touchett gained from his father for Isabel. Significantly, we are told that in anticipating the agreeable consequences of his interview with Mr. Betterman, "Gray had never felt around him any like envelope whatever" (ANS, 907); and Gray's turning over the funds to Horton's disposal thus parallels Isabel's attempt to give Osmond the facticity of money while retaining herself its symbolic potential.

What the outcome of The Ivory Tower would have been is of course a purely speculative matter, and James's elaborately twisting and ruminating Notes, particularly in the light of contradictory developments in what we have of the text, are hardly definitive in providing an answer. But there is some indication that the pattern of The Portrait of a Lady would have been advanced even further and that Gray would find himself culpable, in a sense different from the recognitions of Ralph and Isabel, for having put at Horton's disposal the agency of his corruption. "It has been my idea," James says, "that this 'bad' figures in a degree to Gray as after a fashion his own creation, the creation, that is, of the enormous and fantastic opportunity and temptation he has held out—even though these wouldn't have operated in the least, or couldn't, without predispositions in Horton's very genius" (ANS, 1028). The avoidance of the particularity of "doing," then, would have resulted in "doing" of an even more sinister order, and the network of guilt would have been complete.

The union of money and imagination which ends *The Golden Bowl*, tragic overtones though it may have, seems remarkably, optimistically unlikely as a conclusion for *The Ivory Tower*. No such fusion can exist in Rosanna, for not only does her moral sense make her detest her wealth, but she has no imagination: "With Rosanna he [Gray] isn't going to communicate 'intellectually', aesthetically, and all the rest, the least little bit" (*ANS*, 1010). The imagination of the novel is Graham Fielder's, but its movement toward such a reconciliation is hardly presaged by either the completed portions of the book or the author's *Notes*. Fielder's symbolic retreat into the ivory tower is a movement away from the world of money, though at the same time it is a movement toward the document which reveals the corruption at the base of his inheritance.[7]

Matthiessen's speculations on the book's outcome are intriguing but unconvincing:

> Whether or not Fielder's final illumination in his talk with [Rosanna] is to carry to the length of their marriage, James does not say. But he conceived of his scene as of 'a big and beautiful value,' and it would certainly have symbolized the union between form and spirit, between Fielder's aesthetic perception and her moral massiveness. Perhaps James would also have been able to imagine here a solution for both Rosanna's and Fielder's problems in a free and growing life of culture that had put aside the curse of great wealth.[8]

The major thrust of the "momentous . . . scene" as projected by James is hardly the union Matthiessen suggests but the horror behind the fact of money:

> She goes the whole "figure," as they say, and puts to him that exactly her misery is in having come in for resources that should enable her to do immense things, but that are so dishonoured and stained and blackened at their very roots, that it seems to her that they carry their curse with them, and that she asks herself what application to "benevolence" as com-

> monly understood, can purge them, can make them anything
> but continuators, somehow or other, of the wrongs in which
> they had their origin. This, dramatically speaking, *is* momen-
> tous for Gray. . . . It makes its mark for value, has an effect,
> leaves things not as they were. (ANS, 1012)

The great scene, as postulated, is a further step toward Gray's
complete renunciation, and that such was James's provisional
outcome for the novel is indicated by his saying: "I want Gray
absolutely to inherit the money, to have it, to have had it, and
to let it go" (ANS, 1005).

That the action of *The Ivory Tower* was to transpire not
primarily in Newport but in New York—"the New York world
of business, the N.Y. world of ferocious acquisition, and the
world there of enormities of expenditure and extravagance"
(ANS, 997, 1025)—further supports the novel's documentation
of a collapse of possibility. Much of what James had seen in
America had charmed and delighted him, but these were not
to be the scenes of the action of *The Ivory Tower*. Washington
seemed a consummately social city, a city of conversation; but
that was largely the result of its "indifference to the vulgar
vociferous Market" and the fact that "nobody was in 'business'" (AS, 342, 345). Philadelphia became the antithesis of
New York, and its absence of tall buildings was the symbol of a
social homogeneity which recalled the old Newport or, better,
Europe. "The living fact, in the United States, *will* stand, other
facts not preventing," James felt, "for almost anything you may
ask of it" (AS, 321–322). But other facts did prevent, and the
great American vagueness, when it came to the writing of *The
Ivory Tower*, permitted itself to be read in only one way. The
converting imagination still cherished its belief, but the commerciality of the discovered materials rendered them intractable.

Notes

CHAPTER ONE: *Biographical*

1. Robert C. Le Clair, *Young Henry James: 1843–1870*, p. 376.

2. Jan W. Dietrichson, *The Image of Money*, p. 40.

3. Documented in Leon Edel, *Henry James: The Untried Years*, pp. 19–21, and Le Clair, p. 18.

4. Le Clair, p. 83.

5. See Quentin Anderson's brilliant discussion of the elder Henry James's sense of the "social" in *The American Henry James*, pp. 16–21, 63–82.

6. Quoted in Le Clair, p. 66.

7. *Ibid.*, pp. 83–84.

8. See Dietrichson, pp. 49, 50.

9. Documented fully by Dietrichson, pp. 45 ff.

10. Quoted in F. W. Dupee, *Henry James*, p. 207. Edel's assertion that Mrs. Wharton misunderstood James's "continued ironies about his inability to live up to her style" (*Henry James: The Master*, p. 207) does not, I think, deny a possible financial fear at the base of the irony.

11. See Dietrichson, pp. 68–163.

CHAPTER TWO: *The Early Tales*

1. The financial motif is vaguely present in what is actually James's first published story, the anonymously printed "A Tragedy of Error," which appeared in the February issue of *Continental Monthly* in 1864. The heroine hires an assassin whose pure mercenariness is needlessly emphasized by his complaints of poverty, and the lady's lover offers what is for the rest of James a prophetic bromide: "In life we are all afloat on a tumultuous sea; we are all struggling toward some *terra firma* of wealth or love or leisure . . .

(p. 205). Very little is significant, however, in this fairly pat and sordid little tale, except perhaps the profusion of sea imagery, which will become so important in James's work. Edel documents the authenticity of "A Tragedy of Error" in *Henry James: The Untried Years*, pp. 215–218.

2. As Dietrichson notes (p. 70).

3. James Kraft, however, argues that Theodore is "just as eager for the inheritance, only not as aware of his means of obtaining it" (*The Early Tales of Henry James*, p. 46).

4. Dietrichson, however, attributes her final choice to her discovering "what a fine personality [Crawford] has" (p. 119).

5. *Ibid.*, p. 108.

6. John Bayley, *The Characters of Love*, pp. 161–162, 276.

7. For Dietrichson, she is "clearly mercenary" and "the more immoral of the two" (p. 144).

8. Oscar Cargill points out the similarity of "Longstaff's Marriage" to *The Portrait of a Lady*, but, I think, strains the relationship (*The Novels of Henry James*, pp. 84–85).

CHAPTER THREE: *The Early Novels*

1. As J. L. Ward demonstrates, this pattern of fulfilment for Nora is never integrated with Roger's antithetical and restrictive plan for her (*The Search for Form*, pp. 60–76).

2. Edwin T. Bowden, *The Themes of Henry James*, p. 24.

3. Dietrichson notes this aspect of Newman's naïveté (pp. 138–139). For Edel, "the boorishness in Newman resides not in his pretensions—decidedly superficial—to cultivating art or architecture; it is the side of him which is at once pride in being a 'self-made' man and in his crass unawareness that there are things in the world which cannot be bought" (*Henry James: The Conquest of London*, p. 250). The aesthetic insensitivity and the "crass unawareness" are, however, virtually one.

4. See Bowden, *The Themes of Henry James*, pp. 32–33.

5. Cargill, p. 51.

6. They also foreshadow Osmond and Madame Merle of *The Portrait of a Lady* in their indeterminacy. As Felix categorizes his sister and himself: "You know there are people like that. About their country, their religion, their professions they can't tell" (*Eur*, 28).

7. Richard Poirier, *The Comic Sense of Henry James*, p. 129.

8. *Ibid.*, p. 103.

CHAPTER FOUR: *The Portrait of a Lady*

1. Lyall H. Powers, "*The Portrait of a Lady*: 'The Eternal Mystery of Things,'" *Nineteenth-Century Fiction*, XIV (September 1959), p. 149.

2. As Tony Tanner notes, "while [Isabel] thinks she is ascending toward the world of ends, she is in fact getting more deeply involved in the world of means" ("The Fearful Self: Henry James's *The Portrait of a Lady*," in *Henry James; Modern Judgements*, ed. Tony Tanner, p. 145).

3. This idea is developed convincingly by Poirier, pp. 214–216.

4. Frederick C. Crews, *The Tragedy of Manners*, pp. 13–18.

5. The passage which I have italicized does not appear in the original edition of *The Portrait of a Lady* (Boston, 1881), p. 76.

6. Yvor Winters, *In Defense of Reason*, pp. 308, 310–311.

7. Cargill, p. 82.

8. Poirier's fine discussion of "free" and "fixed" characters throughout *The Comic Sense of Henry James* seems in part marred by a confusion between these two levels.

9. Naomi Lebowitz's interesting, if undeveloped, reference to "the determinism of American romanticism" is to the point (*The Imagination of Loving*, p. 61).

10. Poirier, pp. 7–10. Poirier is as aware as anyone that a novel is a highly selective verbal construct as well as a representation of reality, that it deals in concepts and propositions as well as objects and entities, and that it attempts through language a kind of concrete universality in which, by what amounts to logical trick, the singular experiential data of the work allow the inference of a universal hypothesis from which these data themselves follow—a hypothesis which, I suppose, is what we call theme. The critical trick is to give character and reality their due without slighting the intellectual content, and vice versa, and I am not sure the trick admits of performance, entailing as it does the nature of symbolization (and literary symbolization as distinct from that of ordinary language)—the relation of word to concept, of sentence to proposition.

11. Tanner sees the early Isabel as "an uncommitted, undefined self" ("The Fearful Self," p. 143).

12. David W. Marcell, "High Ideals and Catchpenny Realities in Henry James's *The Portrait of a Lady*," in *Essays in Modern American Literature*, p. 30.

13. As Tanner notes, "The lady is half willing to be turned into a portrait" ("The Fearful Self," p. 147).

14. See Leon Edel, "The Choice So Freely Made," *The New Republic*, 26 September 1955, p. 26; Marion Montgomery, "The Flaw in the Portrait: Henry James vs. Isabel Archer," *The University of Kansas City Review*, XXVI (1960), p. 216; R. W. Stallman, "The House That James Built—*The Portrait of a Lady*," *Texas Quarterly*, I (1958), p. 187; and Walter F. Wright, *The Madness of Art*, p. 147. All these critics see the "carriage" passage as symptomatic of some sort of "flaw" in Isabel and even connect it with her sense of freedom, but none comments on the irony that her freedom is here asserted as a submission to external determination. For Edel the passage simply indicates that Isabel's ideal of happiness is a swift movement into the unknown; for Stallman it characterizes her lack of insight and for Wright her "wilful illusion that life should be recklessly daring." Montgomery sees in it "the romantic expansion of freedom into a vice" and associates it with Isabel's shrinking from knowing what her freedom really is—an interpretation which, in addition to its irrelevant normativeness, falls short basically in begging the question of what the concept of freedom entails in the novel.

15. William H. Gass, "The High Brutality of Good Intentions," *Accent*, XVII (Winter 1958), p. 68.

16. Edwin T. Bowden, *The Dungeon of the Heart*, p. 91. William Bysshe Stein, "*The Portrait of a Lady*: Vis Inertiae," *The Western Humanities Review*, XIII (1959), pp. 178–179.

17. Christof Wegelin, *The Image of Europe in Henry James*, p. 75.

18. Dorothea Krook, *The Ordeal of Consciousness in Henry James*, pp. 33–37.

19. R. P. Blackmur, "Introduction" to *The Portrait of a Lady*, pp. 3, 5.

20. Gass, pp. 68–70.

21. Ernest Sandeen, "*The Wings of the Dove* and *The Portrait of a Lady*: A Study of Henry James's Later Phase," *PMLA*, LXIX (1954), pp. 1061–1064.

22. Ellen Douglass Leyburn emphasizes the role of Ralph's imagination in his misreading of Isabel (*Strange Alloy*, p. 41).

23. This point is argued convincingly by John Rodenbeck in "The Bolted Door in James's *Portrait of a Lady*," *Modern Fiction Studies*, X (Winter 1964–65), pp. 331, 333, 335–336.

24. C. B. Cox, *The Free Spirit*, p. 45.

25. Tanner observers that "perhaps this [Osmond's] apparent lightness, this seemingly empty detachment from the world is more attractive to Isabel than the solid identity, the heavy actuality of Goodwood and Warburton"; but he does not pursue the point ("The Fearful Self," p. 147).

26. It is interesting to note that this passage originally read: "What continued to please this young lady was his extraordinary subtlety. There was such a fine intellectual intention in what he said, and the movement of his wit was like that of a quick-flashing blade" (PL, 242). What the revised image loses in overt presentation of a lurking cruelty it more than gains in subtle thematic portentousness. The related passage (NY, IV:11), quoted below, is also missing from the original (PL, 265).

27. Whether aestheticism is itself necessarily "sterile" in fiction is a significant question raised by John Bayley in his consideration of *The Golden Bowl*: "The assumption that seems to get itself made not only in studies of James but in the criticism of any novelist who explores moral situations [is] that the character who lives in an aesthetic way—that is, makes himself as attractive as he can by means of his appearance, tastes, or status—must necessarily be an inhuman character. It is the kind of convention that would end by making the whole fictional world of moral enquiry quite arbitrary and meaningless, and it is certainly not observed by James, though the character of Gilbert Osmond in *The Portrait of a Lady* is of so clear and straightforward an intention that it has added a lot of weight to the general acceptance of the aesthetic as the automatic adversary in any novel which concerns moral values. In the modern idiom, Osmond is not 'on the side of life', and this is accepted as a characteristic of his aestheticism; but in fact this aestheticism is not necessarily of a piece with the reptilian will and the lack of any sort of generosity which make him such a repellent figure" (p. 224). Certainly what Isabel sees in Osmond, if mistakenly, and what she projects for herself is a continuity of the moral and the aesthetic, and certainly such a continuity is a premise which James puts to the test in each of his novels. There is little question, however, that Osmond's aestheticism takes a sterile, stifling form and that his reification of human beings is associated directly with it, though whether aestheticism is cause, effect, symptom, symbol, or mere contiguous attribute is not quite so easy to assert. The aestheticism of *The Golden Bowl* is, anyway, as Bayley says, a different matter.

28. Tanner points out that "Isabel accepting Osmond's pro-

posal of marriage is the uncertain self thinking it is embracing the very image of what it *seeks* to become" ("The Fearful Self," p. 148).

29. This image, like many others of the same nature, is not in the original edition (*PL*, 285).

30. Lebowitz stresses only the latter conversion in the *Portrait* (p. 84).

31. The question of Isabel's "passion" is a tricky one. Is she frigid, as so many commentators say; and if so, is her frigidity caused (as this passage might suggest) by the fear of an overwhelming sexuality which the right man might unleash? Does she appear undersexed precisely because she is oversexed? James is not very interested in the metaphysics of sexuality in a Nietzschean-Wagnerian-Mannian sense, though Isabel's passivity and her near death-wish at the end of the novel provide us with a rough approximation of that sense. He is extremely interested, however, in the metaphysics of love—in this case, the metaphysical bases for Isabel's conduct in relation to the men with whom she is romantically involved—and to write her off as frigid or James as incompetent in not drawing her motivation as primarily sexual is both to overvalue the necessary simplism of linguistic formulae and hopelessly to underestimate the extremely various and complex human situations which we blanketly term "love."

32. Not surprisingly, the image is missing from the original, in which the pertinent paragraph concludes thus: ". . . the consciousness of what was in her own heart. It was terrible to have to surrender herself to that" (*PL*, 272). James has, in his revision of the *Portrait* for the New York Edition, considerably thickened and complicated the texture and thereby the thematic development of the work by elaborating in tropes Isabel's meditations on her own state—tropes which, more often than not, adumbrate her internal condition in terms of those externals which constitute for Madame Merle the expression and extension of the self but for Isabel the limits upon its freedom. The imagistic density of the revision, which echoes the synthetic mode of the later novels, particularly *The Golden Bowl*, both enriches and renders more problematic the question of the self and its relations, especially as the question appears to Isabel's own confused awareness.

33. Lebowitz, however, suggests the possibility (pp. 82, 84).

34. It might be said that in this similarity the *Portrait* and *The Golden Bowl* differ from *The Wings of the Dove*, where the lines are more clearly drawn and where there is seemingly no such

playing, or (as in *The Golden Bowl*) reversal of roles. However, Milly's silence regarding Densher and her own awareness of how Kate must appear to him is just as marked as Kate's; and her assumption of the parts of the "dove" and "the American girl" is testimony to her command of the false, though saving appearance.

35. Krook, pp. 357–362.

36. As Viola Hopkins Winner notes in her excellent study *James and the Visual Arts*, "The true wisdom of Madame Merle's words is ultimately understood by Isabel. Isabel's life has been a web of relationships rather than the ship with wind in its sails" (p. 141).

CHAPTER FIVE: *The Golden Bowl*

1. Ferner Nuhn, *The Wind Blew from the East*, pp. 130, 138.

2. F. O. Matthiessen, *Henry James: The Major Phase*, p. 90.

3. Bayley, p. 249.

4. F. R. Leavis, *The Great Tradition*, pp. 194–196.

5. Joseph J. Firebaugh, "The Ververs," *Essays in Criticism*, IV (1954). Jean Kimball, "Henry James's Last Portrait of a Lady: Charlotte Stant in *The Golden Bowl*," *American Literature*, XXVIII (January 1957).

6. Miriam Allott, "Symbol and Image in the Late Works of Henry James," *Essays in Criticism*, III (July 1953), pp. 334, 336.

7. Tony Tanner, "*The Golden Bowl* and the Reassessment of Innocence," *London Magazine*, I (November 1961), p. 44.

8. One could demur that Osmond, lacking the means of acquisition, is in far greater need of concealment than Maggie. The issue would then, however, necessarily turn to the world of difference between Isabel and the Prince.

9. Dietrichson points out the Prince's "awareness that he is a valuable item purchased at great cost" (pp. 160–161), and Leyburn notes that "the *sposi* too are parties to the bargains" (p. 66).

10. James's treatment of the Prince seems to cry out for his having read his brother's *Pragmatism*, which was not published until 1907. That the novelist had, as he wrote to William, "unconsciously pragmatised" all his life is at least heartening. See Marius Bewley, *The Complex Fate*, p. 148.

11. Laurence Holland, *The Expense of Vision*, p. 352.

12. Caroline Gordon, "Mr. Verver, Our National Hero," *The Sewanee Review*, LXIII (1955), p. 44.

13. Cargill, p. 438.

14. *Ibid.*, pp. 420, 438.

15. Dorothea Krook, in her intelligent analysis of *The Golden Bowl's* ambiguity, touches on Maggie's questioning of the validity of her hypotheses, though her treatment of the two passages which she cites seems to me in one case to fail to do justice to the complexity of the passage and in the other simply to be wrong (*The Ordeal of Consciousness in Henry James*, pp. 311–313). The first passage is that in which Maggie sees Charlotte approaching her on the terrace and concretizes her fear, in Miss Krook's words, "that Charlotte might go to Adam, tell him openly about Maggie's suspicions of her, and convince Adam that they were wickedly false." The text goes: "Such a glimpse of [Charlotte's] conceivable idea . . . opened out wide as soon as it had come into view; for if so much as this was still firm ground between the elder pair, if the beauty of appearances had been so consistently preserved, it was only the golden bowl as Maggie herself knew it that had been broken. The breakage stood not for any wrought discomposure among the triumphant three—it stood merely for the dire deformity of her attitude toward them" (*GB*, II:246–247). Miss Krook comments: "It is this fear that decides Maggie that she must 'of her own prudence' persuade Charlotte to believe that she has no quarrel with her; and so, 'with a rare contraction of the heart', she proceeds to do so."

Miss Krook's entire line of argument seems to suggest that Maggie's fear rests on the belief that, should Charlotte be confident enough of her husband to report Maggie's suspicions to him, the entire framework of her suppositions would be demonstrated as false. The phrase "dire deformity of her attitude" can, I suppose, be so read, but in the context it seems to generate meanings other than this. The initial ambiguity of attitude is revealed in Maggie's appraisal of Charlotte's hypothetically speaking to Adam: "It would show her as sufficiently believing in her grasp of her husband to be able to assure herself that, with his daughter thrown on the defensive, with Maggie's cause and Maggie's word, in fine, against her own, it wasn't Maggie's that would most certainly carry the day" (*GB*, II:246). Maggie's worrying more over her father's conceivably siding against her than over the pain which Charlotte's accusation of her suspicions would cause him is a lapse in her concern for him which looks forward to the notable anticipation of a "sign" later in the chapter (*GB*, II:252), though the passage could just as well express an altruistic fear of Adam's being trapped by the duplicitous Charlotte.

The major ambiguity, however, attends the phrase "dire deformity," which could mean, just as easily as Miss Krook's reading, that Adam's innocence demonstrates a faith in maintained appearances which forcibly thrusts itself upon Maggie as an attitude for emulation. It is conceivable, too, that Maggie uses "deformity" in a nonnormative sense, in which case she would mean simply that Adam's ignorance of his wife's betrayal leaves him happy and composed (her suppositions up to this point have made out Adam as knowing everything), whereas her knowledge has discomposed and tortured her mind. Moreover, if there is no wrought discomposure among the three, Amerigo and Charlotte again stand together, ranged against her. In short, the passage is not conclusive evidence that Maggie is calling her own hypotheses into doubt.

The second passage which Miss Krook introduces is that in which Maggie listens to her husband's profession, "You've never been more sacred to me than you were at that hour—unless you've become so at this one," and reacts "as if something cold and momentarily unimaginable breathed upon her, from afar off, out of his strange consistency" (GB, II:207).

Miss Krook says: "The . . . words seem to suggest that she has a momentary doubt, very chilling to her, about the validity of the conclusions she has drawn from what the antiquary told her, which she is at that moment imparting to the Prince. If this is what the words mean (and if they do not, it is difficult to know what they do mean), the 'doubt' would clearly not be of the same radical kind as the one cited above." What the words do mean is stated precisely by Laurence Holland: "Her being 'sacred' to him may count for no more than it did before, but his devotion, if genuine and now stronger, is the ground on which she must build" (p. 388).

16. Maxwell Geismar, Henry James and the Jacobites, pp. 309–312.

17. Crews, pp. 94–95.

18. Ibid., p. 95.

19. Nuhn, p. 158.

20. Holland, p. 366.

21. Stephen L. Mooney, "James, Keats, and the Religion of Consciousness," The Modern Language Quarterly, XXII (December 1961), p. 399.

22. Ibid., p. 401.

23. John Henry Raleigh similarly exonerates the Ververs from the charge of acquisitiveness, but his "Lockean" argument for their money's sanctity is quite unfathomable ("Henry James: The Poetics of Empiricism," PMLA, LXVI [March 1951], pp. 111–112).

24. Nuhn, pp. 124–125.

25. Holland, pp. 358–359.

26. Lebowitz notes that Maggie's "innocent 'use' of the Prince made Charlotte's use of her possible" {p. 102).

27. Laurence Holland brilliantly summarizes the effect of the Brighton sequence: "The fantastic scene is powerful because of the many pressures it exerts which contribute to the *funny form* of James's novel. It makes of the fictive courtship and marriage of Adam and Charlotte inside the novel a contorted image of numerous actualities which either do or might exist outside it, all the more contorted an image for the range of its relevance and the variety within the conjunction it forges: conventional marriage as a domestic, sexual, and commercial convenience, deliberately chosen by the partners but subordinating marital to familial and occupational concerns; the traffic of prostitution; the transformation of an ordinary acquisitive enterprise in the realms of business and of taste into a more discriminating, intimate, and viable experience" (p. 363).

28. Cox, p. 68.

29. Bewley, pp. 84, 94.

30. Bayley, pp. 226, 236.

31. Randall Stewart, "The Moral Aspect of Henry James's 'International Situation,'" *The University Review*, IX (Winter 1943), p. 112.

32. Wegelin, p. 136.

33. Cargill, pp. 408–409.

34. Holland, p. 398.

35. Matthiessen, p. 100.

36. H. K. Girling, "The Function of Slang in the Dramatic Poetry of *The Golden Bowl*," *Nineteenth-Century Fiction*, XI (December 1956), p. 146.

37. Bayley, p. 232.

38. Krook, p. 273.

CHAPTER SIX: *The Ivory Tower*

1. Winters, p. 315; see also p. 311.

2. See Newton Arvin, "Henry James and the Almighty Dollar," *Hound and Horn*, VII (April–May 1934), pp. 438–442; Marius Bewley, *The Eccentric Design*, pp. 245–258; and Bradford A. Booth, "Henry James and the Economic Motif," *Nineteenth-Century Fiction*, VIII (1953–54), pp. 141–150.

3. Bewley, *The Eccentric Design*, p. 251.

4. Matthiessen, p. 120, citing *AS*, 210.

5. Dietrichson, p. 90.

6. Anderson, p. 326.

7. James seems to have renounced, in writing the book, the plan sketched in the *Notes* of having Davey Bradham reveal to Gray his uncle's shady financial dealings (ANS, 1005, 1011). Rather, James seems to have left the revelation to a letter of Abel Gaw's, sealed up by Gray in the ivory tower, which object is never mentioned in the *Notes*. Horton's suggestion that Gaw leaves Gray "the great Rosanna" in the letter (ANS, 971) is unlikely.

8. Matthiessen, p. 129.

Bibliography

1. Works by Henry James.

The American. Boston: James R. Osgood and Company, 1877.

The American Novels and Stories of Henry James. Edited by F. O. Matthiessen. New York: Alfred A. Knopf, 1947.

The American Scene. New York: Charles Scribner's Sons, 1946.

Autobiography. Edited by F. W. Dupee. New York: Criterion Books, 1956.

Eight Uncollected Tales of Henry James. Edited by Edna Kenton. New Brunswick: Rutgers University Press, 1950.

The Europeans. London: Macmillan and Company, 1921

The Golden Bowl (in two volumes). New York: Charles Scribner's Sons, 1904.

A Landscape Painter. New York: Scott and Seltzer, 1919.

The Madonna of the Future. London: Macmillan and Company, 1888.

Master Eustace. New York: Thomas Seltzer, 1920.

The Novels and Tales of Henry James: The New York Edition (in twenty-four volumes). New York: Charles Scribner's Sons, 1907–1909.

The Portrait of a Lady. Boston: Houghton Mifflin and Company, 1881.

Roderick Hudson. Boston: James R. Osgood and Company, 1876.

Selected Fiction. Edited by Leon Edel. New York: E. P. Dutton and Company, 1953.

Stories Revived (in three volumes). London: Macmillan and Company, 1885.

"A Tragedy of Error," Continental Monthly, V (February 1864): 204–216.

Travelling Companions. New York: Boni and Liveright, 1919.

Watch and Ward, Longstaff's Marriage, Eugene Pickering, and Other Tales. London: Macmillan and Company, 1923.

II. *Critical Studies*

Allott, Miriam. "Symbol and Image in the Late Works of Henry James," *Essays in Criticism*, III (July 1953):321–336.

Anderson, Quentin. *The American Henry James*. New Brunswick: Rutgers University Press, 1957.

Arvin, Newton. "Henry James and the Almighty Dollar," *Hound and Horn*, VII (April–May 1934):434–443.

Bayley, John. *The Characters of Love*. New York: Basic Books, 1960.

Bewley, Marius. *The Complex Fate*. London: Chatto and Windus, 1952.

———. *The Eccentric Design*. New York: Columbia University Press, 1963.

Blackmur, R. P. "Introduction" to *The Portrait of a Lady*. New York: Dell Publishing Company, 1961.

Booth, Bradford A. "Henry James and the Economic Motif," *Nineteenth-Century Fiction*, VIII (1953–54):141–150.

Bowden, Edwin T. *The Dungeon of the Heart*. New York: Macmillan Company, 1961.

———. *The Themes of Henry James*. New Haven: Yale University Press, 1956.

Cargill, Oscar. *The Novels of Henry James*. New York: Macmillan Company, 1961.

Cox, C. B. *The Free Spirit*. London: Oxford University Press, 1963.

Crews, Frederick C. *The Tragedy of Manners: Moral Drama in the Later Novels of Henry James*. New Haven: Yale University Press, 1957.

Dietrichson, Jan W. *The Image of Money*. Oslo: Universitetsvorlaget, 1969.

Dupee, F. W. *Henry James*. New York: William Sloan Associates, 1951.

Edel, Leon. "The Choice So Freely Made," *The New Republic*, 26 September 1955, pp. 26–28.

———. *Henry James: The Untried Years: 1843–1870*. Philadelphia: J. B. Lippincott Company, 1953.

———. *Henry James: The Conquest of London: 1870–1881*. Philadelphia: J. B. Lippincott Company, 1962.

———. *Henry James: The Master: 1901–1916*. Philadelphia: J. B. Lippincott Company, 1972.

Firebaugh, Joseph J. "The Ververs," *Essays in Criticism*, IV (1954):400–410.

Gass, William H. "The High Brutality of Good Intentions," *Accent*, XVIII (Winter 1958):62–71.

Geismar, Maxwell. *Henry James and the Jacobites*. Boston: Houghton Mifflin Company, 1963.

Girling, H. K. "The Function of Slang in the Dramatic Poetry of *The Golden Bowl*," *Nineteenth-Century Fiction*, XI (December 1956):130–147.

Gordon, Caroline. "Mr. Verver, Our National Hero," *The Sewanee Review*, LXIII (1955):29–47.

Holland, Laurence Bedwell. *The Expense of Vision*. Princeton: Princeton University Press, 1964.

Kimball, Jean. 'Henry James's Last Portrait of a Lady: Charlotte Stant in *The Golden Bowl*," *American Literature*, XXVIII (January 1957):449–468.

Kraft, James. *The Early Tales of Henry James*. Carbondale: Southern Illinois University Press, 1969.

Krook, Dorothea. *The Ordeal of Consciousnes in Henry James*. Cambridge: Cambridge University Press, 1962.

Leavis, F. R. *The Great Tradition*. Garden City: Doubleday and Company, 1954.

Lebowitz, Naomi. *The Imagination of Loving: Henry James's Legacy to the Novel*. Detroit: Wayne State University Press, 1965.

Le Clair, Robert C. *Young Henry James: 1843–1870*. New York: Bookman Associates, 1955.

Leyburn, Ellen Douglass. *Strange Alloy: The Relation of Comedy to Tragedy in the Fiction of Henry James*. Chapel Hill: University of North Carolina Press, 1968.

Marcell, David W. "High Ideals and Catchpenny Realities in Henry James's *The Portrait of a Lady*," in *Essays in Modern American Literature*, pp. 26–34. Deland: Stetson University Press, 1962.

Matthiessen, F. O. *Henry James: The Major Phase*. New York: Oxford University Press, 1963.

Montgomery, Marion. "The Flaw in the Portrait: Henry James vs. Isabel Archer," *The University of Kansas City Review*, XXVI (1960):215–220.

Mooney, Stephen L. "James, Keats, and the Religion of Consciousness, *The Modern Language Quarterly*, XXII (December 1961):399–401.

Nuhn, Ferner. *The Wind Blew from the East*. New York: Harper and Brothers, 1942.

Poirier, Richard, *The Comic Sense of Henry James*. New York: Oxford University Press, 1960.

Powers, Lyall H. "*The Portrait of a Lady*: 'The Eternal Mystery of Things,'" *Nineteenth-Century Fiction*, XIV (September 1959):143–156.

Raleigh, John Henry. "Henry James: The Poetics of Empiricism," *PMLA*, LXVI (March 1951):107–123.

Rodenbeck, John. "The Bolted Door in James's *Portrait of a Lady*," *Modern Fiction Studies*, X (Winter 1964–65):330–340.

Sandeen, Ernest. "*The Wings of the Dove* and *The Portrait of a Lady*: A Study of Henry James's Later Phase," *PMLA*, LXIX (1954):1060–1075.

Stallman, R. W. "The Houses That James Built—*The Portrait of a Lady*," *Texas Quarterly*, I (1958):176–196.

Stein, William Bysshe. "*The Portrait of a Lady*: Vis Inertiae," *The Western Humanities Review* XIII (1959):177–190.

Stewart, Randall. "The Moral Aspect of Henry James's 'International Situation,'" *The University Review*, IX (Winter 1943): 109–112.

Tanner, Tony. "The Fearful Self: Henry James's *The Portrait of a Lady*." In *Henry James: Modern Judgements*, edited by Tony Tanner, pp. 143–159. London: Macmillan and Company, 1968.

———. "*The Golden Bowl* and the Reassessment of Innocence," *London Magazine*, I (November 1961):38–49.

Ward, Joseph L. *The Search for Form: Studies in the Structure of James's Fiction*. Chapel Hill: University of North Carolina Press, 1967.

Wegelin, Christof. *The Image of Europe in Henry James*. Dallas: Southern Methodist University Press, 1958.

Winner, Viola Hopkins. *Henry James and the Visual Arts*. Charlottesville: University Press of Virginia, 1970.

Winters, Yvor. *In Defense of Reason*. New York: Swallow Press and William Morrow and Company, 1947.

Wright, Walter F. *The Madness of Art*. Lincoln: University of Nebraska Press, 1962.

Index